PROJECT FIELDWORK

BRIAN GREASLEY

UNWIN

HYMAN

Published by
Unwin Hyman Limited
15–17 Broadwick Street
London W1V 1FP

First published in 1984 by
University Tutorial Press Limited
Reprinted 1986, 1987, 1988

ISBN 0 7135 2675 0

Printed in Great Britain at
The University Press, Cambridge

TO THE STUDENT

Probably the most enjoyable part of geography is fieldwork. All geography must at one time have started with someone doing some fieldwork – finding out what a place is like, and about the people who live there. The world is an exciting place and there is no need to travel far from home to find fieldwork opportunities. Topics for investigation are all around us, whether we live in urban or rural areas.

However, there is little point in undertaking a lengthy investigation unless you are well prepared and know what you are doing. This book sets out to explain exactly how a field investigation should be undertaken. You should take careful note of the early sections about choosing a topic and developing an idea to test, and the final section on writing up and presenting your work. The central section of the book explains methods of investigating a variety of topics and shows how the results can be analysed and presented.

The book contains a lot of ideas for investigation and methods which you could try. However, it is *your* idea and the methods *you* use which are important. The book is there to help you, may all go well!

TO THE TEACHER

An increasing number of teachers and examination courses are requiring students to undertake investigative fieldwork. The approach may be new to many students who are inclined to undertake descriptive rather than investigative work. This book attempts to make the students in the 14–16 age range aware of the investigative method. To this end it is divided into broad sections relating to choosing a topic, developing a suitable hypothesis, methods of testing that hypothesis, analysing the results, writing a conclusion and presenting the finished work.

The techniques described are those which have proved reliable in practice. The range includes those which may be used in connection with physical and human topics in both rural and urban environments.

The book is written for the student and is designed for a wide ability range. With a variety of topics, the flexible approach allows the student to choose those sections which are relevant. Alternatively, there is material which could be used for class teaching, many sections containing exercises which are designed to enable the student to become familiar with techniques before embarking on a study.

It is intended that this book should be available during the period when the student is undertaking fieldwork, providing a source of information to enable that work to be undertaken successfully.

ACKNOWLEDGEMENTS

The author and publishers are grateful to the following for the use of illustrative matter:
Fig 1.4 Countryside Commission; Fig 2.1 (left) David McKie, *The Guardian*; Fig 2.1 (centre) copyright *Music Week*/BBC/Gallup; Fig 2.1 (right) Dennis Barker, *The Guardian*; Figs 3.4 & 3.5 Hanwell JD and Newson MD, *Systematic Physical Geography*, Macmillan, London and Basingstoke; Fig 3.17 Rona Mottershead, TGOP No. 23 'Practical Biogeography', The Geographical Association; Fig 3.28 Briggs D, *Sediments*, Butterworth; Fig 3.31 reproduced from Census 1981 Small Area Statistics with the permission of the Controller of Her Majesty's Stationery Office. Crown Copyright Reserved; Fig 3.53 Eastern Counties Omnibus Co Ltd; Figs 4.3 & 4.7 Robin M Haynes et al. 'Community attitudes towards accessibility of hospitals in West Norfolk' in Malcolm J Moseley (ed) *Social Issues in Rural Norfolk* (Centre of East Anglian Studies 1978); illustration on page 130 Lesley Burgess; illustration on page 131 Alistair Smith; base maps on pages 26 (two), 65, 78 & 103 reproduced from the Ordnance Survey with the permission of the Controller of Her Majesty's Stationery Office, Crown Copyright Reserved; base map on page 72 Woodspring District Council Leisure and Tourism Department; base map on page 125 Michael Young for the Ely Society. Despite every effort, the publishers have been unsuccessful in seeking permission to reproduce Fig 3.45, believed to be by George Ferris in *Classroom Geographer* (Jan 1982). They ask the author/publisher to contact them should this book succeed in coming into their hands.

We would also like to thank the following for the use of photographs: pages 5, 23, 24, 39, 101 (four) J Allan Cash Ltd; pages 12, 16 (left), 67 (top two), 68, 70 (six), 76, 81 (two), 99 George Williams; page 44 Paul Cleves; page 95 *Cambridge Evening News;* page 109 Eastern Counties Omnibus Co Ltd; page 133 Mike Petty, the Cambridgeshire Collection. All other photographs were taken by the author.

For B 'a very human geographer . . . '

CONTENTS

PART 1: THE APPROACH

Fieldwork   1–2
This book   3–4
Fieldwork is . . .   5–6
An idea to test? – the choice   7–8
An idea to test? – now break it up!   9–10
The question 'why?'   11–12
Before you go . . .   13–14

PART 2: TO COLLECT THE DATA

To collect the data   15–16
Sampling   17–18
Questionnaires   19–22
What the eye sees?   23–24
Maps   25–26
The library   27–28

PART 3: COLLECT AND RECORD

PHYSICAL GEOGRAPHY TOPICS

Weather studies   29–33
What happens to rain?   34–38
Slopes   39–41
Soils   42–44
Vegetation   45–47
Rivers and streams   48–52
The sea and the shore   53–54
On the beach   55–56

HUMAN GEOGRAPHY TOPICS

Counting people   57–58
More people   59–61
The village   62–64
The village grows and changes   64–68
Patterns in towns – growth   69–71
Patterns in towns – land use   71–73
Patterns in cities   74–76

In the centre   76–82
Retailing   83–84
The town and beyond   85–86
Rural land use   87–88
On the farm   89–90
The world of work   91–92
The place of work   93–94
Transport – traffic in town   95–96
Transport – out of town   97–98

ENVIRONMENTAL TOPICS

How do we see places?   99–100
The quality of rural and urban environments   101–102
Streetscapes   103–104
Pressures on the countryside   105–106

PART 4: PROCESSING AND PRESENTING THE DATA

What is the most usual number? – the mean, median and mode
                                                           107–108
Graphs and charts – the bar chart, histogram and pie chart 109–111
Around the centre – star diagrams and radial charts   112–114
Finding the connection: 1 – the scattergraph   115–116
Finding the connection: 2 – correlation   117–118
Mapping   119–121
How many are there? – dot and density maps   122–124
Line maps – isoline maps   125–126
Mapping flows   127–128

TESTING THE HYPOTHESIS

The final act   129–130
Completion and general presentation   131–132

SOURCES OF INFORMATION

Sources of information   133–134

FIELDWORK

Have you ever wondered why that one patch in the school field is always flooded when it rains, while the rest drains easily? Whether the stones in a stream are the same size in every part of it? Why the shops in a village are closing down? How and why the way people use the land varies from one field to the next? Or how the local park is used?

To find the answers to all these questions and many more, geographers go out into the town, city or countryside for fieldwork visits. Fieldwork is finding out about the real world for ourselves. Books can tell people the answers to some questions, but they do not give the answers to questions about small areas.

The only way to find out the answers to questions about the school playing field or the local park or shopping centre is to go and find out. Sometimes geographers will go to new areas to test ideas in new situations. Perhaps a suitable stream is not to be found near home and the geographer needs to travel to more distant places.

Wherever it may be, in the local area or far from home, geographers are trying to test ideas and get answers to questions by finding out at first hand.

Those taking part in fieldwork need to plan their investigation to make it worthwhile. Even if their fieldwork is to be carried out near to home they need to know what equipment to take with them. When they return, they need to know how to use the information they have collected and write up the results.

EQUIPMENT

The equipment needed will vary, depending upon whether the day's investigation is to take place indoors or outdoors or in an urban or rural area. Suggestions for the equipment needed for outdoor fieldwork are shown here.

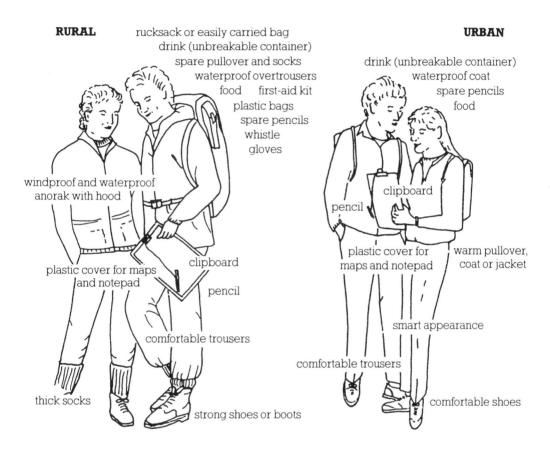

RURAL

rucksack or easily carried bag
drink (unbreakable container)
spare pullover and socks
waterproof overtrousers
food   first-aid kit
plastic bags
spare pencils
whistle
gloves

windproof and waterproof
anorak with hood

plastic cover for maps
and notepad

clipboard

pencil

comfortable trousers

thick socks

strong shoes or boots

URBAN

drink (unbreakable container)
waterproof coat
spare pencils
food

clipboard

pencil

plastic cover for
maps and notepad

warm pullover,
coat or jacket

smart appearance

comfortable trousers

comfortable shoes

Fig 1.1 EQUIPMENT FOR RURAL AND URBAN FIELDWORK

GOLDEN RULES FOR RURAL FIELDWORK

Always tell someone where you are going

Never go to high moorland without an experienced adult

Never go alone – go with a friend or in a group

EQUIPMENT CHECKLIST

RURAL FIELDWORK

Clothing to wear
- warm, comfortable clothes
- windproof and waterproof anorak and hood
- comfortable trousers
- thick socks
- strong shoes or boots

In the rucksack
- waterproof trousers
- food
- drink (in unbreakable container)
- spare pullover and socks
- first-aid kit
- whistle
- gloves
- spare pencils and sharpener

To carry
- clipboard and pencils
- maps
- plastic cover for clipboard

URBAN FIELDWORK

Clothing to wear
- comfortable clothes
- warm pullover, coat or jacket
- comfortable trousers
- comfortable shoes

In the rucksack or bag
- waterproof coat
- spare pencils and sharpener
- food
- drink (in unbreakable container)

To carry
- clipboard and pencils
- plastic cover for clipboard

THIS BOOK

This book is designed to provide help in the planning of a fieldwork investigation. Good planning not only produces a more satisfying piece of work but saves time and effort on the way.

AN IDEA TO TEST (pages 7–10) explains how to choose a topic for study and how that topic may be broken down into testable ideas. Examples are given at each stage to help the explanation. These examples show how to approach the chosen topic.

TO COLLECT THE DATA (Part 2) outlines the types of data which may be collected. Many of the examples given link with the ideas given in the previous section. Page numbers (in brackets) make reference easy, so that an idea may be followed up.

COLLECT AND RECORD (Part 3) suggests ways in which the data may be collected and recorded. This part is divided into three sections: one for topics in Physical Geography, one for Human Geography and one for Environmental topics. You can select the section(s) you require for your own particular topic.

The next part, headed PROCESSING AND PRESENTING THE DATA (Part 4), explains what to do with the information once it has been collected. It is worthwhile looking at this when planning what data to collect.

Finally, the section TESTING THE HYPOTHESIS (pages 129–32) explains how to complete the writing up of the investigation.

It is worthwhile looking at all the sections which are relevant to your investigation before you do any fieldwork. This may well save time which might otherwise be wasted in collecting information which cannot be used.

Everyone who undertakes fieldwork is involved in a unique piece of work. This book explains how to approach it and gives examples. But because each piece of work is unique and belongs to the person undertaking it, this book cannot explain exactly what to do in every circumstance, but it can help.

FIELDWORK IS . . .

TOURISTS WINDOW SHOPPING IN WOODSTOCK, OXFORDSHIRE

Fieldwork is collecting information. Good fieldwork is collecting information for a purpose. There are two main reasons why geographers need to collect information. One is to test whether an idea they have had is correct. The second is to find the answer to a question which they have asked as a result of reading or something they have seen.

For instance, they might want to know why the larger villages in an area of beautiful countryside are always so crowded. Do the people who have come to shop in the village all live locally? Or are they all visitors? If they are visitors, have they or do they intend to tour the countryside? Why are they attracted to this particular village? Are they aware that large numbers of people crowding into a village, and the amenities provided for them, may make the village less attractive? These and many other questions arise from the first simple question.

An investigation into an idea like this should be as organised as possible. There are a series of steps to follow:

 1 The idea which is to be investigated should be written down. For instance: 'People visiting areas of beautiful countryside collect in large villages, requiring amenities which may change the villages' character.'

 2 If this statement is to be tested, there are several questions which need answering, such as those which were asked earlier. These questions should be written out clearly.

3 Having decided on the questions which need answering, it is necessary to decide for each question:

(a) what information is to be collected in order to provide the answer.

(b) how that information is to be collected, e.g. from a local library, by asking people a series of questions, or by observation.

Often it will be necessary to visit the area to collect the information. A feeling for what the place is like and what its special features are can also be gained from a visit.

 4 The information can now be collected together and processed. This may mean collecting it together in the form of maps, graphs or figures, or in some other way so that it may be easily understood. The outcome of this is that the data will be displayed or presented so that others may see the results.

 5 The statement or idea can now be tested. The fieldwork results can be used to answer the individual questions which were asked, and then the main statement may be tested.

 6 The statement may need modifying in some way, in which case a new statement may be written out and conclusions drawn.

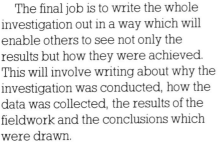

STEPS TO TAKE

THINK OF AN IDEA TO TEST

PRODUCE SEVERAL TESTABLE
IDEAS OR QUESTIONS

COLLECT THE DATA

PROCESS THE DATA

PRESENT THE DATA

TEST THE IDEA

WRITE A
CONCLUSION

The final job is to write the whole investigation out in a way which will enable others to see not only the results but how they were achieved. This will involve writing about why the investigation was conducted, how the data was collected, the results of the fieldwork and the conclusions which were drawn.

The investigation will be unique; no one else will be able to repeat it (for instance, on the same day and in the same conditions), so it is worth taking care at each stage.

AN IDEA TO TEST? – THE CHOICE

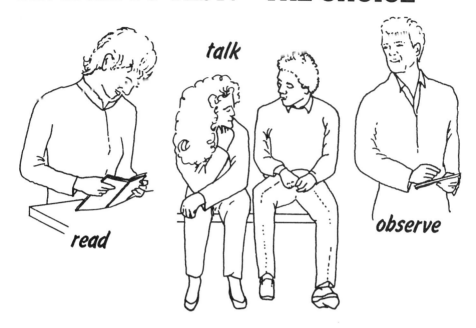

Fig 1.2 MAKING THE CHOICE

When there is the chance to do some fieldwork there is always the question of 'What am I going to investigate?'. Sometimes the answer is obvious – often a topic for investigation is given, but equally often there is a free choice.

Whatever the situation, it is important to think carefully about which topic to choose. It should be something which interests the investigator. For instance, it may be that a person is interested in athletics, visits a stadium regularly for training, and wants to find out the effects of events at the stadium on the surrounding area. Are there problems of congestion and car parking in nearby streets? How wide is the area affected by the noise from the stadium? Which are the main routes followed by the spectators to and from the stadium? These and many other questions would form the basis of an investigation.

If a person is interested in what they are doing, then that interest will help to overcome the problems they may face. This is important, as there are likely to be times when some tedious work needs to be done. Following something of interest helps to make the work original. There is no sense of satisfaction to be gained from copying someone else unless it is testing the idea in a new area.

It is important not to be too grand or ambitious in the choice of topic. Small, straightforward and simple ideas often produce the most interesting fieldwork and provide the most satisfying results.

The topic chosen should be geographical – after all this is to be a piece of geographical fieldwork. This is not as much of a restriction as it may sound for much of what happens in the world has a geographical element.

The investigation should be worthwhile. It is more satisfying to carry out an investigation which has a purpose. In the investigation of the effects of events at a stadium, the results could form the basis of a discussion on how to lessen those effects.

What of the information which needs to be collected? It may take some time to complete the investigation; will the material be available for that length of time? Can the information be obtained relatively easily? Many industries, large stores and farmers, for instance, may not wish to give details of their concerns.

It may be that a person is asked to complete an investigation, but an idea is not well formed in their mind. In this case it would be advisable to go to the library and look through some books which may help give an idea. Talking ideas over with someone, preferably a teacher (but it perhaps helps to start with a friend), can help to clarify those ideas. It is also worth going to look round the area in which the investigation is to take place. In the example this would be the area around the stadium, the best time being on the day of an event. Thinking in odd moments about the investigation also helps to gradually form ideas.

THE CHOICE – QUESTIONS TO ASK YOURSELF

If the answer is 'Yes', go ahead. If an answer is 'No', then think again.

		Yes	No
1	Am I interested in what I propose to do?	☐	☐
2	Is what I propose geographical?	☐	☐
3	Will the information be available when I need it?	☐	☐
4	Is what I propose worthwhile?	☐	☐
5	Is what I propose simple and not too ambitious?	☐	☐
6	Is what I propose original?	☐	☐
7	Have I read about what I propose in books?	☐	☐
8	Have I talked over my ideas with others?	☐	☐
9	Have I observed the area in which I want to work?	☐	☐
10	Have I thought in detail about what I propose?	☐	☐
11	Am I clear in my own mind about what I aim to do?	☐	☐

AN IDEA TO TEST? NOW BREAK IT UP!

Think about your idea

Produce a question or statement

Break it up into small manageable pieces

The best kind of fieldwork is that which starts by either asking a question or making a statement. For instance, a question may be asked such as, 'Does the angle and aspect of a slope affect land use?' or, 'Are there more pedestrians on one side of the High Street because Marks and Spencer is on that side?'. Each of these questions could be thought of as a statement: for instance, 'The angle and aspect of a slope affects land use' or, 'There are more pedestrians on one side of the High Street than the other because Marks and Spencer is on that side'.

It does not matter whether the idea is written as a question or as a statement, as long as it is clear and concise. To arrive at that point will have taken a considerable amount of time and discussion. Now the statement needs to be broken down into a series of testable sections which will form the basis of the study. These sections will be tested by the data collected out in the field.

In the case of the question, 'Does the angle and aspect of a slope affect land use?', it will be necessary to choose a slope to investigate. Obviously one cannot work on a large variety of slopes and it may well be that a slope in the local area is the one in which the fieldworker is interested. The questions that then arise are: What is the angle of the slope? Is the angle of the slope uniform or does it vary with height and at different positions along the slope? What is the aspect of the slope? Does the aspect vary at different positions along the slope? What is the land use at different points along the slope? All these questions point to the need for deciding how and where the measurements are to be taken (see Sampling, pages 17–18). Finally, if this investigation does show that angle and aspect affect land use, then it would be useful for the fieldworker to try to find out why this is so.

The statement that 'There are more pedestrians on one side of the High Street than the other because Marks and Spencer is on that side' does involve finding out the reasons if it proves correct. In this case the statement may be broken down into a series of statements for testing. For example, 'There are more pedestrians on one side of the High Street than the other'; here the investigator will need to decide when to survey the number of pedestrians. If it is correct that most of the pedestrians are on the same side as Marks and Spencer then a statement like, 'The main reason is that Marks and Spencer is on the side with the most pedestrians' will need to be tested. Mapping the amenities and shops in the area of the survey may show that there are other possible reasons, as may a questionnaire to shoppers.

1   In discussion with a friend, try to break up the following ideas into testable statements. Remember to think about what the investigator needs to know in order to test the idea.

'The pebbles found in the deeper sections of a stream are smaller than those in the shallow sections.'

'Does the quality of the environment improve with distance from the city centre?'

'Is the effect of an event taking place at a stadium only felt along the lines of the main roads, and does it decrease with distance from the stadium?'

'Antique shops cluster together in the historic areas of a town.'

THE QUESTION 'WHY?'

Why are you doing this?

At all stages of an investigation the fieldworker should be asking the question, 'Why?'. One of the first questions the fieldworker should ask is, 'Why am I doing this?'. The answer should be, 'To test . . .' or, 'To find out . . .'. If the fieldworker feels that the work is worthwhile, then the result will be worthwhile. The question, 'Why?' makes the fieldworker think about what is being done in a purposeful way.

If the fieldworker is involved in an investigation into the pedestrian flow along a street, the first problem encountered is when should the fieldwork be carried out. A short period of observation would soon show that the flow of people along a street varies through the day. There will be fewer people in the early morning or evening than in the middle of the day, and there will be virtually no-one at night. The flow will also vary during the week.

A second question that will arise is where to stand in the street. This will be particularly important if there are other streets joining the main street at different intervals.

The answers to these problems are for the fieldworker to decide. Each street is different – a special set of circumstances occurs in each instance. What is important is that the decision that is made is one which is made for a reason or set of reasons. The reasons for the decision should then be outlined in the field notebook and final write-up of the investigation.

Such justification of the decisions that are taken should be clear at each stage of the investigation: deciding when and where to carry out the fieldwork; deciding which method of collecting data to use; and deciding how to collect the data (parts 2 and 3) and how to process it (part 4). If the reasons are given at each stage then the investigation is much less open to criticism and much more likely to be successful.

WHERE WOULD YOU STAND?

1 Why is it necessary to decide when to carry out a pedestrian flow count? (See also pages 79–80.) When would *you* carry out a pedestrian count in the centre of your local town or city?

2 Why is it important to decide where to stand to carry out a shopping questionnaire survey? (See also pages 19–22.) Where would *you* stand to carry out such a survey in your own town or city centre?

BEFORE YOU GO . . .

The work done before the investigator goes into the field can save an enormous amount of time and effort. Being poorly equipped or poorly informed can lead to countless problems and even to the whole visit having to be abandoned.

It is worth spending time obtaining as much information on the topic being studied as possible. If someone else has done a similar study then it is worthwhile learning from their mistakes. Information about the area being visited, from maps, guidebooks, as well as textbooks, all helps. Discussing the project with an experienced fieldworker can also be invaluable.

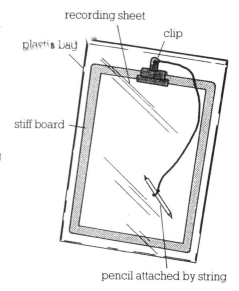

Fig 1.3 A CLIPBOARD

If a particular aspect of the work being undertaken does not lend itself to testing by the methods described in this book or elsewhere, perhaps these methods can be adapted. There are ways round most problems. Each piece of fieldwork is different and presents its own difficulties; the good fieldworker can find a way!

Collecting material together well beforehand avoids forgetting items which later prove essential. For work in the field a clipboard on which to write is essential. A pencil can be tied to it with string by cutting a groove at one end of the pencil; if it is sharpened at both ends, there is a second point if one breaks. A pencil sharpener should be carried as well as a rubber (which could also be tied to the clipboard). A protective cover will help to protect the work in case of rain; a transparent plastic bag would do, although it is possible to buy a map case. Spare pencils, a watch and a compass are essential for rural fieldwork. A shoulder bag or rucksack to carry things in will leave hands free.

All fieldworkers should have a notebook and a map of the area. As well as the date and time of the investigation, the notebook will carry all the information collected and notes on anything which is relevant to the work. The pages should be marked up before the fieldworker sets out, so that everything is ready when the recording is started.

Other equipment being taken will depend on the topic being investigated, but a checklist should be drawn up beforehand and checked before setting out. There is nothing worse than reaching a site and being unable to proceed because a vital piece of equipment is missing. It is also well worth testing equipment before setting out. Trying an experiment in the school grounds or in the garden can help to eliminate faults, show what is possible, and help to make the fieldworker familiar with the equipment before it is used for 'real'.

Finally, a word about permission – if at any stage the investigation involves moving from public highways or paths onto private land, then it is vital that permission has been obtained beforehand. A polite letter to the owner usually brings a satisfactory response, as long as it is written at least a fortnight in advance to give time for a reply.

WHEN YOU GO . . .

There are two major points for the fieldworker to remember when undertaking fieldwork. The first is to be accurate and to record carefully. Often it will not be possible to return to the site and find conditions which are exactly the same. Details cannot be remembered afterwards. Good recording, although it takes a little longer in the field, saves an enormous amount of time afterwards.

The second point is that the investigation should cause as little interference with the lives of others as possible. It always pays dividends to be polite. In rural areas it is essential to adhere to the Country Code. Always tell someone where you are going; if anything happens, someone will know where you will be. Finally, money for a phonecall has often saved a long walk home when a bus has been missed!

Enjoy the countryside and respect its life and work.

Guard against all risk of fire.

Fasten all gates.

Keep your dogs under close control.

Keep to public paths across farmland.

Use gates and stiles to cross fences, hedges and walls.

Leave livestock, crops and machinery alone.

Take your litter home

Help to keep all water clean.

Protect wild life, wild plants and trees.

Take special care on country roads.

Make no unnecessary noise.

Fig 1.4 THE COUNTRY CODE

1 Write out a checklist of equipment needed for a day's fieldwork investigating land use in:
(a) a town (pages 71–73 may help)
(b) a rural area (pages 87–88 may help).

TO COLLECT THE DATA

WHAT TYPE OF DATA IS BEING COLLECTED IN EACH OF THESE FOUR PHOTOGRAPHS?

The data required to test ideas or questions will depend very much on the type of idea or question being tested. It is most important that the data collected is relevant and that it is capable of providing sound evidence for the study. There are two types of data that can be collected, that from primary sources and that from secondary sources.

Data from **primary sources** is obtained from personal observations made in the field. This type of data may include surveys, questionnaires, photographs, field sketches, sketch maps, transects, measurements and interviews – indeed any data collected at first hand. This is an essential part of fieldwork and many people find it the most interesting. There are a variety of techniques which may be used to collect data from primary sources and many of them are outlined in this part of the book and in Part 3: Collect and Record.

Data from **secondary sources** is material collected by others and made available usually as printed material. This type of data includes books, magazines, articles, directories, government statistics, company publications, newspapers, television, radio and maps. Such

information may not only be used as data for testing but also for providing a comparison. For instance, secondary data would provide historical information on the extent, population and occupations of a village. This could be compared with primary observations in the field and used to illustrate the changes which have taken place there.

The choice of what data to collect should be considered carefully. It could be the case that an idea would need to be modified or even abandoned if relevant information were not available.

Sometimes too much information is available. For instance, a fieldworker studying the effect of aspect and slope on land use finds that a particularly rare flower grows on the slope being studied and that the area has been designated as a nature reserve. The fact that it is a reserve and its effect on land use would be interesting and useful. However, there is little point in spending a great deal of time discovering the finer points of the vegetation found in the reserve, even though there may be a wealth of material available.

The data chosen must provide good evidence for the study. If a study is being made of the effects of a bypass on a town, then evidence of the traffic flow before the road was built may be difficult to find. Snippets of conversation with a few people will not provide a sound basis for a comparison.

Finally, always check that data can be processed satisfactorily. Part 4 of this book will help and should be looked at before a final decision about what data to collect is made.

SAMPLING

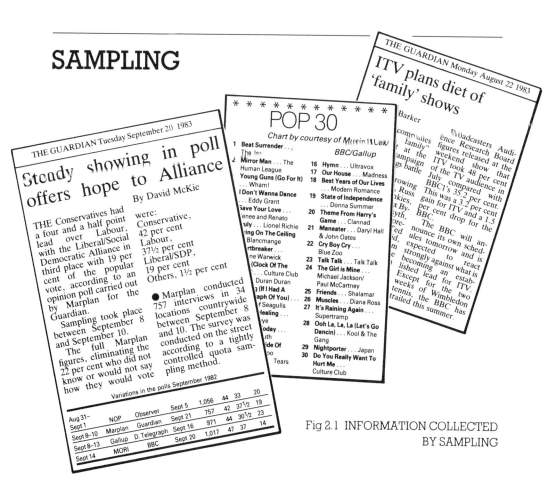

THE GUARDIAN Tuesday September 20 1983

Steady showing in poll offers hope to Alliance

By David McKie

THE Conservatives had a four and a half point lead over Labour, with the Liberal/Social Democratic Alliance in third place with 19 per cent of the popular vote, according to an opinion poll carried out by Marplan for the Guardian.

Sampling took place between September 8 and September 10.

The full Marplan figures, eliminating the 22 per cent who did not know or would not vote how they would vote

were:
Conservative, 42 per cent
Labour, 37½ per cent
Liberal/SDP, 19 per cent
Others, 1½ per cent

● Marplan conducted 757 interviews in 34 locations countrywide between September 8 and 10. The survey was conducted on the street according to a tightly controlled quota sampling method.

Variations in the polls September 1982

				1,056	44	33	20
Aug 31–Sept 1	NOP	Observer	Sept 5				20
Sept 8–10	Marplan	Guardian	Sept 21	757	42	37½	19
Sept 8–13	Gallup	D. Telegraph	Sept 16	971	44	30½	23
Sept 14	MORI	BBC	Sept 20	1,017	47	37	14

THE GUARDIAN Monday August 22 1983

ITV plans diet of 'family' shows

...Barker

...companies ...at the ...campaign ...gs battle

...rowing ...Russ ...nkies, ...x By- ...yth- ...ore- ...ed ...id, ...m ...e

ence Research Board figures released at the weekend show that ITV took 48 per cent of the TV audience in July compared with BBC1's 35.2 per cent. This was a 3.2 per cent gain for ITV and a 1.5 per cent drop for the BBC.

The BBC will announce its own schedules tomorrow and is expected to react strongly against what is becoming an established lead for ITV. Except for the two weeks of Wimbledon tennis, the BBC has trailed this summer.

POP 30

Chart by courtesy of Music Week

BBC/Gallup

1 Beat Surrender . . . The Jam
2 Mirror Man . . . The Human League
   Young Guns (Go For It) . . . Wham!
   I Don't Wanna Dance . . . Eddy Grant
   Save Your Love . . . Renee and Renato
   uly . . . Lionel Richie
   ing On The Ceiling . . . Blancmange
   rtbreaker . . . ne Warwick
   (Clock Of The . . . Culture Club
   Duran Duran
   g (If I Had A aph Of You) . . .
   f Seagulls
   ealing . . .
   ye
   oday . . .
   uth
   de Of
   po
   Tears

16 Hymn . . . Ultravox
17 Our House . . . Madness
18 Best Years of Our Lives . . . Modern Romance
19 State of Independence . . . Donna Summer
20 Theme From Harry's Game . . . Clannad
21 Maneater . . . Daryl Hall & John Oates
22 Cry Boy Cry . . . Blue Zoo
23 Talk Talk . . . Talk Talk
24 The Girl is Mine . . . Michael Jackson/Paul McCartney
25 Friends . . . Shalamar
26 Muscles . . . Diana Ross
27 It's Raining Again . . . Supertramp
28 Ooh La, La, La (Let's Go Dancin) . . . Kool & The Gang
29 Nightporter . . . Japan
30 Do You Really Want To Hurt Me . . . Culture Club

Fig 2.1 INFORMATION COLLECTED BY SAMPLING

How is the information like that shown above collected? Is everyone in the country asked which television programmes they watch, or which political leader they support? Is every record shop asked for a return of the numbers of records sold? The answer is no, they are not. It would be impossible to collect evidence from everyone. Therefore a few people are chosen to represent everyone. This is known as sampling. The more people chosen, the more accurate the result will be.

This technique is very useful if a large area, a large number of people, or a long time period is involved. For example, if a study were being made of how infiltration rates (i.e. how quickly water soaks into the ground) vary over the school playing field, then it would be necessary to know where to position the cans (into which water is poured to measure how quickly it soaks away over a given time). It is not possible to place cans all over the field. One method might be to position the cans at random over the field (Fig 2.2A). Another method might be to position them at measured regular intervals over the field (Fig 2.2B). Alternatively it might be worthwhile putting them in a line across the field (Fig 2.2C). In each case the

---

results would represent the whole area. Perhaps it is known that the underlying rock types vary over the area. If one third of the area were of rock type X and two thirds of type Y, it might be best to make sure that one third of the sample were on rock X and two thirds on rock Y.

Similar techniques can be used when surveys involving people are being undertaken. Not everyone can be questioned if work is being undertaken into the trade area of a shopping centre. A sample taken at random for two hours may result in a preponderance of one type of person. For instance, if a weekday is chosen then senior citizens, who are not working and who are most willing to stop, may make up the bulk of the sample (see next section on questionnaires). One way around this problem could be to observe the types of people using the centre and make up a sample according to the number of people of each type.

Surveys of all kinds pose similar problems. The time at which the sample is taken may prove vital. In the case of traffic surveys, with variations through the day and week, careful thought about when to conduct a count is important.

The key to success is to decide how the sample is to be chosen, with clear reasons for the choice. Discussing the choice with others can only help. Once a choice has been made for good reasons, there should be no need to change the method once collecting has started. The results will be accurate and should not be changed even if they are unexpected.

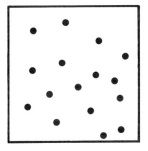

A: RANDOM SAMPLING

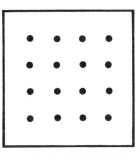

B: SYSTEMATIC POINT SAMPLING

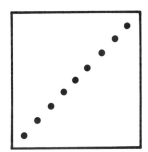

C: LINE SAMPLING

Fig 2.2 TYPES OF SAMPLING

1   Read the information in Fig 2.1. What kind of sample was taken by the Marplan Poll of Sept. 8–10, published in *The Guardian* on Sept. 20?

2   (a) What kind of sample would be taken if any person passing by were questioned at a shopping centre?
    (b) What kind of sample would be taken if every tenth person passing by were questioned at a shopping centre?

QUESTIONNAIRES

A questionnaire involves asking people a series of questions. Questionnaires are not only time consuming, they involve the goodwill of other people and many groups find them essential. Too many investigators asking questions could antagonise people and make the job of someone else very difficult. *Only use a questionnaire if it is the only possible way to obtain the information required.*

When constructing a questionnaire it is important that:

1 Only questions which will gain relevant information should be included. The shorter the question, the better it is. No one likes to be kept standing on a cold and windy pavement answering long lists of questions.

2 The questions must be analysed afterwards. The easiest type to analyse are those where a tick is placed in a box, or the answer is yes or no. This is straightforward if you are simply asking for factual information. Question 1 in questionnaire A uses this method, and is much better than asking, 'How often do you visit Castleton?'.

Asking for an opinion is more difficult; merely to say, 'Do you think this is an attractive village?' will bring a host of replies which will be difficult to analyse. By asking this in the way Question 5 in questionnaire A does, the responses can be analysed easily.

It may be necessary to ask which features the person finds most attractive or unattractive. In this case a list of possibilities could be given, perhaps with a blank at the end in case the person being interviewed wants to include an extra feature. (See Question 4 in questionnaire A.) The person could be asked to rank a number of alternatives in order of importance. (See Question 6 in questionnaire A.)

A WELL CONDUCTED QUESTIONNAIRE

QUESTIONNAIRE A

Date .... Time..

Could you help me – I am conducting a survey into aspects of tourism in the village and wondered if you would mind answering a few questions.

1 Do you visit Castleton – more than once a month? ☐
– once a month? ☐
– 2 or 3 times a year? ☐
– less than once a year? ☐

2 Do you live – in Castleton? ☐
– within one mile of Castleton? ☐
– between 1 and 5 miles of Castleton? ☐
– between 5 and 15 miles of Castleton? ☐
– more than 15 miles from Castleton? ☐

3 Could you tell me what kind of work you do? ....

4 Are you visiting Castleton now to – shop for groceries? ☐
– shop for gifts or souvenirs? ☐
– visit a cafe? ☐
– look round the village? ☐
– visit a friend? ☐
– for other reasons? ☐

5 Do you find this village – very attractive? ☐
– quite attractive? ☐
– average? ☐
– unattractive? ☐
– very unattractive? ☐

6 Could you put the following features of Castleton in order of their attractiveness? – the buildings ☐
– the surroundings ☐
– the shops ☐
– the peace and quiet ☐
– the amenities provided ☐
– others ☐

That is the last question – thank you for your help.

3 Some questions may be of a personal nature; these should be avoided if possible. Rather than ask the age of a person, the interviewer should have a series of categories and make a judgement. If it is important to know where people live, then it is better to ask for the village or street in which they live, rather than the actual house. If these questions are in the middle of the questionnaire and a friendly relationship has been established, then they are more likely to be answered. (See Question 3 in questionnaire A. Why should the interviewer need to ask this question?)

4 The layout of the questionnaire is very important. Short and clear questions help to ensure that no misunderstandings occur. Questions involving politics, religion or race should be avoided as they could well antagonise people. The layout should be clear and easy to fill in.

5 Finally, some general advice:

(a) A suitable time should be chosen to conduct the questionnaire – half-day closing is no time to be conducting a questionnaire into shopping habits.

(b) A suitable place should be chosen. The best places are where there is a wide pavement and where there are likely to be a lot of people.

(c) People are amazingly friendly when a stranger smiles and speaks politely. It helps to be interested in what people are answering, but the interviewer should not show any expression, for example of surprise, at the answers being given.

(d) It may help to include on the questionnaire a first sentence to help with approaching people.

(e) A good cross section of people should be chosen – senior citizens are often very willing to stop and talk, but the investigation would not be evenly balanced if they were the only group asked (see previous section on sampling).

(f) If someone who is approached does not wish to be interviewed, they should not be asked again but left and someone else approached.

(g) The interviewer should always fill in the questionnaire so that there is no possibility of mistakes.

(h) The interviewer should always look efficient and well organised – with a clipboard and at least two pencils in case one breaks. People are much more likely to be willing to help if the interviewer is someone who is sensibly dressed and looks as if they are doing a serious piece of research.

(i) Sometimes people give obviously ridiculous answers – in this case it is best to finish the survey and then disregard that sheet.

(j) Always thank the person afterwards for taking part. It may be useful to talk to them about their views, but do this at the end of the questionnaire.

Questionnaire B should be read in connection with ideas suggested on page 83.

QUESTIONNAIRE B

Date ....   Time...

Could you help me – I am conducting a survey into aspects of shopping in the area and wondered if you would mind answering a few questions.

1 Are you shopping at this centre today?   Yes
                                                No

2 Do you come here to shop – more than 3 times a week? ☐
                                  – 2 or 3 times a week? ☐
                                  – once a week? ☐
                                  – 2 or 3 times a month? ☐
                                  – once a month? ☐
                                  – less than once a month? ☐

3 Did you travel here today – on foot? ☐
                                – by bicycle? ☐
                                – by car? ☐
                                – by bus? ☐
                                – other ☐

4 Could you tell me which street or road you live in? ....

5 Did you come here to buy items such as groceries,   Yes
       cigarettes, stamps etc.?   No

6 Do you come here to buy clothes or electrical goods?   Yes
                                                             No

       If no, where do you go to buy clothes or electrical goods? ....
       ....

7 Do you come here to buy furniture and carpets?   Yes
                                                        No

       If no, where do you go to buy furniture and carpets? ....
       ....

8 Could you choose the three factors from the following list
       which best describe why you use the centre for shopping?
                                          – near home ☐
                                          – good car parking ☐
                                          – friendly shops ☐
                                          – cheap prices ☐
                                          – good amenities ☐
                                          – not crowded ☐
                                          – other ☐

That is the last question – thank you for your help.

WHAT THE EYE SEES?

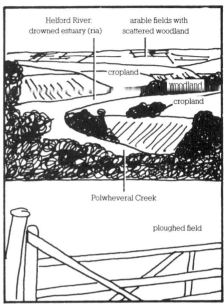

Fig 2.3 PHOTOGRAPH AND SKETCH OF A LANDSCAPE

Sometimes it may be necessary to record what the landscape in a rural area or townscape in an urban area looks like. For instance, studies concerned with physical features, environmental aspects of the landscape or townscape, or leisure use of the land, could benefit from the use of a sketch or photograph.

A photograph, whilst relatively easy to take, will show all the aspects of the view. It will not separate out the geographical features which the fieldworker may wish to emphasise. Views which involve distant objects or landscape are very difficult to take successfully. Often the main object of concern is so far away and appears so small that the photograph is of little value. If photographs are used to reveal aspects, then the fieldworker should note carefully the point from which the picture was taken and the direction the camera was pointing. When used, the picture should be fully labelled so that the particular features being displayed are clear.

Field sketching requires some practice but even those with little artistic talent can produce a worthwhile sketch. By drawing the horizon and the main features first, then filling in the sketch, the major geographical aspects of the view may be shown. The most important point to remember about field sketching is to concentrate on the geographical features and not worry too much about unnecessary detail. As with photography, labelling can help to bring out the point the fieldworker is trying to show.

PHOTOGRAPH FOR USE WITH QUESTIONS 1 AND 2

An alternative is to draw a circle or arc divided into three divisions to represent the near, middle and far distance of the view. In each division are placed the headings which are thought to be important and detail recorded under these headings (see Fig 2.4). This method cannot replace the sketch but may be used as a record of a viewpoint for future use, or as additional material.

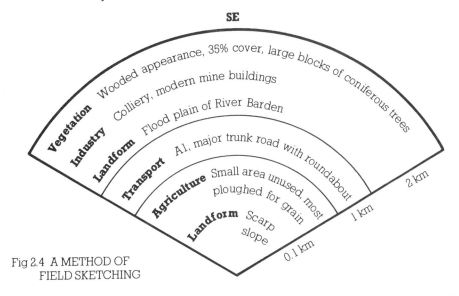

Fig 2.4 A METHOD OF FIELD SKETCHING

1 Use the photograph at the top of this page to draw a sketch to show the main features of the landscape.

2 Use the same photograph to record the information using the method suggested in Fig 2.4.

MAPS

Maps form the basis of much work geographers do in the field. Whether it is a large scale plan or a small scale map of an area, the map is often vital to the success of the work.

There are a wide variety of maps to choose from; the local library and local collection will have a copy of many of them. It is important to choose the right map for the job in hand. The most useful maps are usually found to be those produced by the Ordnance Survey, the main map makers in Britain. They produce maps at a variety of scales – 1:1 250, 1:10 000, 1:25 000, and 1:50 000 may prove to be the most useful.

Maps at 1:1 250 scale show details of streets and individual buildings in towns. Such maps would prove useful for marking on information relating to buildings within an urban area (for example, shop types, building materials, land use, etc.). In rural areas, maps at this scale do not show a very wide area, but they do show great detail and may be useful if a small area were being surveyed.

For rural areas, particularly if the fieldworker were walking across an area, maps at scales of 1:10 000 and 1:25 000 may well prove to be the most useful. Such maps would show field boundaries over quite a wide area and the detail is such that features may be accurately located. For urban areas such maps show a broad pattern of land use. For some cities the Ordnance Survey produce City Maps at 1:10 000 scale which show streets and broad patterns of land use: these may prove more valuable.

The maps at 1:50 000 scale are often used, but only for large scale studies; they cover a wide area and detail is very generalised. The Ordnance Survey produce a wide variety of historical and specialist maps: for example, geological maps. (There are also land use maps produced for some parts of Britain.) One advantage of this organisation's maps is that they can be used to trace changes over time. Many local collections have Ordnance Survey maps going back over 100 years, so changes may be traced.

In addition, there are a wide range of locally produced maps and plans which may prove useful. Before starting the fieldwork, it is well worth going to see what is available and choosing carefully the best one for the work being undertaken.

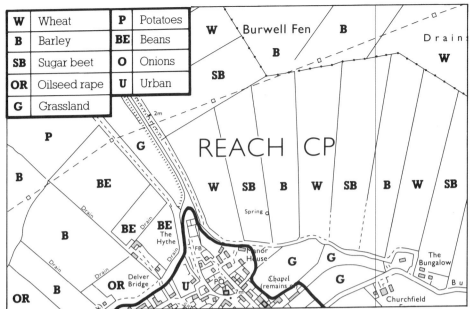

W	Wheat	**P**	Potatoes
B	Barley	**BE**	Beans
SB	Sugar beet	**O**	Onions
OR	Oilseed rape	**U**	Urban
G	Grassland		

Made and compiled by Ordnance Survey Southampton.

CROP SURVEY PLOTTED ON A 1:10 000 SCALE MAP

Made and compiled by Ordnance Survey Southampton.

IW	Inter war housing (1918–39), detached and semi-detached	**R**	Recreation	**S**	Shop
ST	Small terraced pre World War 1 housing	**LT**	Large terraced pre World War 1 housing		
H	Hotel, boarding house, public house	**C**	Commercial (**CB** bank, **CG** garage)		

BUILDING SURVEY PLOTTED ON A 1:2 500 SCALE MAP

THE LIBRARY

INTERVIEWER

Do you only have books here?

It depends what you mean by books; we have books of statistics, directories and magazines here.

And maps?

Our maps are kept in the Local Studies section; most large towns and cities have a collection of materials of general interest about the local area.

When someone comes here for materials, how can you help them?

The most important thing is that they know what they want. We cannot help if they simply ask for all we have on a topic. This may run into numerous files and books, maps and photographs which would take weeks to sort through.

What should they ask for?

They should come with a particular fact or set of facts in mind which they need: figures of employment in villages for instance, or material relating to the quality of housing in an area, for example census material.

So if I were tackling a project, I should come when I need something definite?

Well, yes . . . you could come before to look at what we have and it may be worth checking that we have specific material before you start.

I see – do I need to copy out all the material I find?

We have a photocopy service here – there is a charge – but it does mean you can take some of the data away with you. We are always pleased to help with research, and although much of our material is historical we usually manage to find what is needed.

LIBRARIAN

All towns and cities have one or more libraries. The bigger libraries contain a lending library, a separate reference library, and often a collection of materials about the local area. Books cannot be borrowed from a reference library or local collection, but they can be read at the tables provided.

There is a whole range of published material which may help with a study. Much of this material may be in the form of statistics. These can be rather time consuming to go through for what is needed. They may also be rather complicated. The advice of someone like a teacher or librarian may be of real help and may save a lot of time.

Many books are written about the local area. Some of them may be relevant to a study. They should be used with care. Large sections should not be copied from them. If they are especially relevant and are quoted, they should be acknowledged. At the end of a piece of work all such material should be listed (see page 132).

WEATHER STUDIES

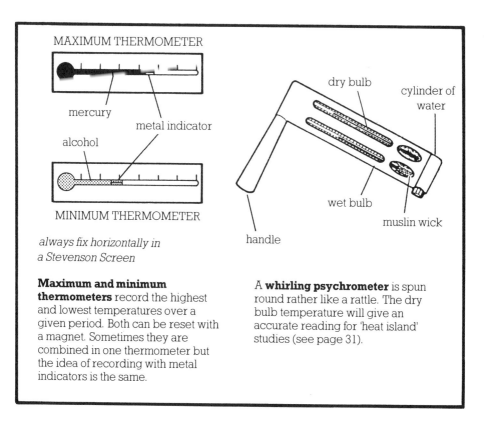

MAXIMUM THERMOMETER

mercury

metal indicator

alcohol

MINIMUM THERMOMETER

always fix horizontally in a Stevenson Screen

dry bulb

cylinder of water

wet bulb

muslin wick

handle

Maximum and minimum thermometers record the highest and lowest temperatures over a given period. Both can be reset with a magnet. Sometimes they are combined in one thermometer but the idea of recording with metal indicators is the same.

A **whirling psychrometer** is spun round rather like a rattle. The dry bulb temperature will give an accurate reading for 'heat island' studies (see page 31).

Fig 3.1 RECORDING THE TEMPERATURE

When people are outside at break or dinner time at school it is well worth watching where they are standing, sitting or playing. On a cold winter's day people may be huddled in groups on one side of the buildings, and on a hot summer's day they may be sitting beneath trees or on another side of the buildings. Can you guess at some of the reasons why the pattern of where people position themselves varies between winter and summer or even from one day to the next?

One of the main reasons will be the weather; they may be sheltering from the cold winter wind or sitting in the shade of a tree in summer. Although there are a large number of weather stations in the British Isles, they cannot give details of the weather for every smallest part of the country. They may provide a picture of the weather over the area as a whole but the weather can change quite dramatically within quite short distances. One side of a hedge or building may

The Beaufort Scale

Beaufort number	Wind	Observation	Speed (km/hr)
0	Calm	Smoke rises vertically	–
1	Light air	Smoke drifts	1–6
2	Light breeze	Leaves rustle	7–12
3	Gentle breeze	Leaves move	13–18
4	Moderate breeze	Small branches move	19–30
5	Fresh breeze	Small trees sway a little	31–40
6	Strong breeze	Large branches sway	41–51
7	Moderate gale	Whole trees sway	52–60
8	Fresh gale	Twigs break off trees	61–74
9	Strong gale	Large branches blown down	75–86
10	Whole gale	Trees uprooted, buildings damaged	87–100
11	Storm	Widespread damage	101–115
12	Hurricane	Disastrous results	over 115

A **weather vane** will show wind direction, which is always given as the direction from which it blows.

An **anemometer** will give wind speed. A simple home-made wind speed indicator is shown. The card swings according to the wind strength. The scale is marked by observation, using the Beaufort Scale.

thick wire

scale

swinging card

sturdy base

Fig 3.2   RECORDING THE WIND

have a very different weather pattern to another side. Investigating such changes, and perhaps coming to some conclusions about the reasons for them, can provide an interesting topic for study.

It is possible to compare observations of a home or school weather station with those of a local station manned by the 'professionals'. Alternatively, readings over a relatively short time period of a few days or weeks could be compared with the passage of weather systems, noting the changes for instance in cloud type and cover, temperature, pressure, wind and humidity.

Whatever type of study is undertaken, it will involve the use of instruments. These may be available at school or it may be possible to make your own. Some are shown above (Figs 3.1 and 3.2). The instrument used will depend on the study being undertaken. Having thought out the study and read about the topic, it would be a good idea to ask for advice about the instruments available and the best ones to use.

Many weather studies can be undertaken around the school or home. Weather study on such a small scale is called micro-climatology. Such studies are easier to handle and require less elaborate instruments than large scale studies.

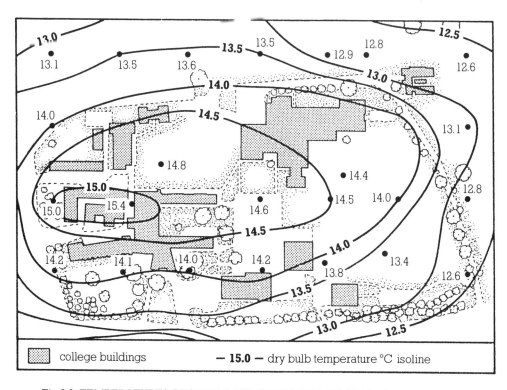

Fig 3.3 TEMPERATURES AROUND IMPINGTON VILLAGE COLLEGE, 28 APRIL 1983

One such study might be to investigate changes in temperature around the school and to test the idea that 'temperature declines with distance from the school buildings'. The fact that temperature might decline more rapidly in different directions would provide an idea for enlarging the study. This investigation could be carried out by taking the temperature at predetermined positions around the school. Decisions need to be taken about the sampling method to be used (see pages 17–18): for instance, would a traverse (i.e. taking readings in a line across the area) be more useful than taking readings at random or at regular intervals? Further, the type of instrument used should be considered: a whirling psychrometer (using the dry bulb only) is recommended for taking accurate readings. The readings may be recorded on a map or numbered key with linked references to the map; the final presentation of data could be produced in the form of an isoline map (see Fig 3.3 and page 126).

Buildings, particularly if they are tall and grouped closely together, can have a marked effect on the velocity (speed) and direction of the wind. Trees and hedges in rural areas, in a garden or in school grounds, can have a similar effect. Once the idea or question to be tested has been formulated and the sampling method decided, then the way in which evidence is to be collected and recorded needs to be discussed. Wind velocity may be measured using an anemometer. One method of measuring direction is to mark at each sample spot the points of the compass with chalk. (A board with directions marked on it could be used on a grass area.) Having the points marked saves the tedious job of deciding the direction each time measurements are taken. The more compass points used, the more accurate the results will be. Talcum powder sprinkled from a container or hand-held paper streamers will indicate the wind direction. Results could be recorded on a table and transferred to a wind rose or a wind star (see page 112). It must be remembered that it will be necessary to compare the direction of the 'free wind' away from the buildings or obstructions.

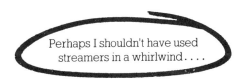

Perhaps I shouldn't have used streamers in a whirlwind. . . .

Many studies are undertaken which investigate the whole climate of a very small area. For example, it is possible to study the different climates on either side of a wall, or around a house, or simply to see how the climate varies with distance from a wall. Such studies may be carried out during one day, or week, or month or year. The whole range of weather instruments would be involved and would need to be positioned carefully.

In all studies of this kind, success will depend not only on the care with which the work has been thought out, but also on the accuracy of the readings. Some of the differences may only be slight, so care with reading and recording is essential.

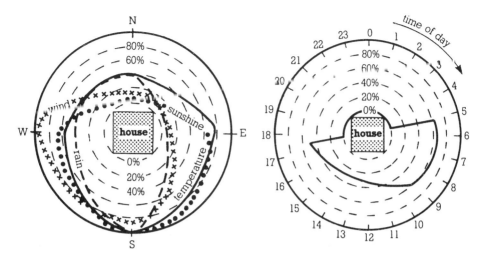

Fig 3.4 CLIMATE AROUND A HOUSE FOR TWO WEEKS IN JULY

Fig 3.5 RECEIPT OF BRIGHT SUNSHINE TO THE WALLS OF A HOUSE FOR TWO WEEKS IN JULY

1 Join with your neighbour and imagine that you have decided to attempt a study concerning the effects of buildings on the velocity and direction of the wind. Answer the following:

(a) State the idea to test.

(b) Break the idea into testable parts.

(c) Outline the sample method you would use to find the position of each measurement.

(d) For how long would the investigation be undertaken?

(e) How often would readings be taken?

(f) How would you decide on when to undertake the study?

(g) Which instruments would you use?

(h) How would you obtain the instruments when you required them?

(i) How would you record the information in your notebook?

2 Carry out the same exercise for a study of one of the following:

(a) temperature differences between north and south facing slopes.

(b) temperature differences between slopes of different angles.

(c) differences in sunshine levels received by the walls of a house.

(d) differences in rainfall within a given area.

WHAT HAPPENS TO RAIN?

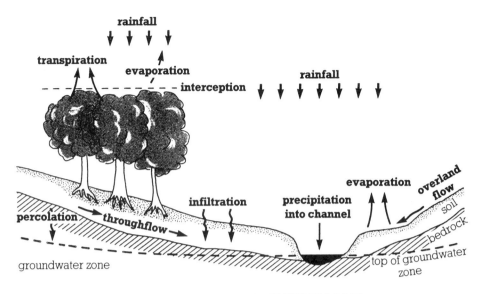

Fig 3.6 THE THINGS THAT HAPPEN TO RAIN

The diagram above shows what happens to rainfall. Many of the processes can be measured using relatively simple equipment and can form the basis of a fieldwork investigation.

PRECIPITATION

Rainfall, or more correctly precipitation, may be measured using a rain gauge. It is possible to purchase a rain gauge and the school may well have one available. But as several rain gauges may be required for the investigation, a funnel and bottle as shown in the diagram will be adequate. A measuring cylinder graduated in millimetres can be used to measure the precipitation collected and the amount of rainfall can be calculated using the formula:

$$\text{precipitation (mm)} = \frac{\text{volume}}{r^2} \text{ (amount of rainfall collected, mm}^3\text{)}$$
(r is the radius of the funnel in mm)

Variations in rainfall at various localities within the school grounds or garden area could form one study, which could be elaborated by investigating the effects of obstructions and wind direction.

INTERCEPTION

The diagram shows that not all the rain which falls reaches the ground; some of it is intercepted by vegetation. Rain gauges set at intervals around a tree (see Sampling, pages 17–18), with one monitoring the uninterrupted rainfall in an open space nearby, would provide evidence. This line of enquiry could be extended by investigating the amount of rainfall intercepted by different types of tree, at different times of year, and how the amounts vary with the intensity of the rainfall. The intensity of rainfall (mm/hr) is the total uninterrupted rainfall (mm) divided by the duration of rainfall (hours).

$$\text{intensity (mm/hr)} = \frac{\text{gross rainfall (mm)}}{\text{duration of rainfall (hr)}}$$

If this investigation were attempted, it would need to be done for individual rain storms.

STEMFLOW

Some of the precipitation reaches the ground as stemflow (flowing down the trunk of a tree or stem of a plant). This is difficult to measure but it can be done by cutting out a plastic bowl or bucket to fit round the base of the trunk, sealing the spaces with Plasticine or waterproof silicone rubber and leading a tube from the bowl to a collecting container.

EVAPORATION

Evaporation may be measured using an evaporation pan consisting of a straight sided bowl with a ruler fixed vertically to the inside of it. For direct comparison the pan should be placed next to a rain gauge. Put some water in the pan (approximately 100 mm) and take the measurement. After a time interval (e.g. one day) note the water level. If no rain fell between readings the evaporation will be the difference between the two readings. For instance, on Day 1 in the table (Fig 3.7): evaporation = [water in pan at start (a) − water in pan after 24 hours (b)] = [100 − 80] = 20 mm.
On Day 2 rain fell, and so evaporation = [(a) − (b)] + precipitation (c) = [100 − 110] + 30 = 20 mm.

Notice that the evaporation pan is refilled after each reading. The evaporation rate may be compared with maximum temperature, number of sun hours, wind speed and other aspects of daily weather.

	(a) Water in pan at start	(b) Water in pan after 24 hrs	(c) Precipitation
Day 1	100 mm	80 mm	0 mm
Day 2	100 mm	110 mm	30 mm

Fig 3.7 EVAPORATION READINGS

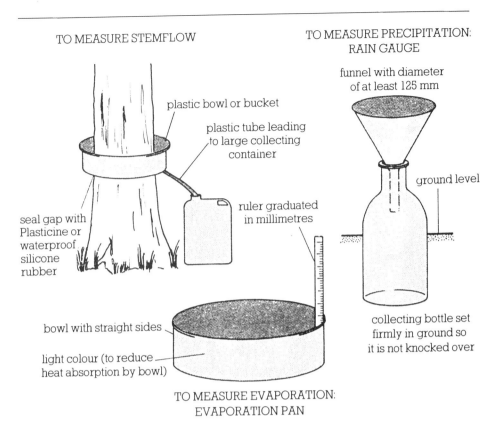

TO MEASURE STEMFLOW

plastic bowl or bucket

plastic tube leading to large collecting container

seal gap with Plasticine or waterproof silicone rubber

TO MEASURE PRECIPITATION: RAIN GAUGE

funnel with diameter of at least 125 mm

ground level

collecting bottle set firmly in ground so it is not knocked over

ruler graduated in millimetres

bowl with straight sides

light colour (to reduce heat absorption by bowl)

TO MEASURE EVAPORATION: EVAPORATION PAN

Fig 3.8 MEASURING EQUIPMENT

INFILTRATION RATES

Most of the precipitation will reach the ground surface. It will then move into the soil either through cracks in the soil, through root holes, through the burrows of creatures like worms or into the pores of the soil itself. This process is known as infiltration. The infiltration rate is the rate at which the rainfall can be absorbed into the soil and is measured in centimetres per minute. The rate usually decreases during a storm until a fairly stable rate is attained.

The infiltration rate may be measured using a large tin (a coffee tin is ideal), with the bottom cut out of it with a can opener. Select a site – this will depend upon the idea you are testing – and push one end of the can about 10 cm into the ground. You may need to clear some litter from the site, but the soil should be disturbed as little as possible. Place a ruler marked in millimetres inside the can at one side (it could be fixed to the can) and mark one point some 5 cm above the ground surface and another approximately 10 cm above the surface.

USING INFILTRATION EQUIPMENT

The next stage is to fill the can to the 10 cm mark. As this is done, make a note of the time the experiment started and start a stopwatch to time the rate at which the water is absorbed into the soil. When the water level reaches the 5 cm mark make a note of the time on the stopwatch and then fill the can to the 10 cm mark and try to keep it there. After one minute stop the supply of water, allowing the level to drop to the 5 cm mark again, recording the length of time taken with the stopwatch. Keep repeating this at regular intervals until the rate at which the water level drops slows down: it may then be repeated at less frequent intervals. Stop the experiment when the rate at which the water level is dropping is constant.

Tuesday 26 July 1983   West Hill, Barton

Site A

Time from start (mins)	Time for water to drop 5 cm (secs)
0	5
1	10
2	20
3	40
4	60
5	70
10	80
15	85
20	90
25	90
30	90

Fig 3.9 INFILTRATION RATES
RECORDED IN A FIELD NOTEBOOK

The page from a field notebook (Fig 3.9) shows a set of recorded results. These can be changed to rate per minute:

Infiltration rate per minute (cm/min) =

$$\frac{5 \text{ cm}}{\text{Time taken to drop 5 cm}} \times 60$$

e.g. 10 mins from start (see notebook page) infiltration rate is:

$$\frac{5}{80} \times 60 = 3.75 \text{ cm/min}$$

The results may then be represented with a line graph.

This method of collecting information on infiltration rates may be used to compare rates in different soil types, in soil with differing vegetation cover, and in soil with differing land use.

SOIL MOISTURE CONTENT

It is also possible to test soil moisture content. Having cleared the litter horizon (i.e. the material on the surface of the soil), take a sample of soil (approximately 200 g) in a sealed airtight container. Push the container into the soil, trying to disturb the soil as little as possible. Clean the outside of the container and in the laboratory weigh the container and soil. Open one end of the container and dry the soil in an oven for about 24 hours at a relatively low temperature (100°C) so that organic material is not burnt. Once the soil is dry let it cool and, taking the soil from the container, weigh the soil and the container separately.

TO FIND THE SOIL MOISTURE CONTENT:

(a) Find the weight of the wet soil (weight before heating of soil and container − the weight of the container).
(b) Find the weight of the dry soil.
(c) Find the weight of the water (i.e. weight of wet soil − weight of dry soil).
(d) Soil moisture content = $\dfrac{\text{weight of water}}{\text{weight of wet soil}} \times 100$

(Answer as a percentage.)

---

1 Write down three ideas you could test involving infiltration rates in the school grounds or a nearby park.

2 Write down three ideas you could test involving soil moisture content in your local area (hints: soil type, vegetation cover, slope).

3 Draw a graph to show the infiltration rates at Site A at West Hill, Barton, shown opposite. (You will need to find the rate per minute first.)

SLOPES

The photograph shows how one side of a valley may differ from the other side. Similar differences may be found on each side of a hill. The soils, vegetation, climate and land use may differ on different parts of a hillside. If you were to undertake an investigation into these differences, the first job would be to find out more about the slope.

The formation of slopes takes place over a long period of time and is often very complicated. One would need to look elsewhere for information and it is perhaps better to leave such an investigation until later.

There are, however, three features of a slope which can be studied and measured without needing complicated pieces of equipment: they are height, aspect and the angle of steepness.

Height may be found by looking at the contour lines or spot heights on a large scale Ordnance Survey map.

The aspect of a slope is the direction in which the slope is facing. This may affect vegetation and land use: south facing slopes receiving the direct rays of the sun for long periods are warmer than other slopes, particularly those which face north. Aspect may be found by standing at different points on a hillside and using a compass to find direction. However, slopes may well be uneven and minor variations may occur. As it is not possible to measure every inch of the slope, some form of sampling is needed (see pages 17–18).

Similarly a method of sampling will need to be chosen when finding the angle of steepness of the slope. The steepness may well affect a whole range of features which could be studied in association with slopes (e.g. soils, vegetation). Two methods of measurement are described below, each of which require instruments which it is quite possible to make.

USING A CLINOMETER

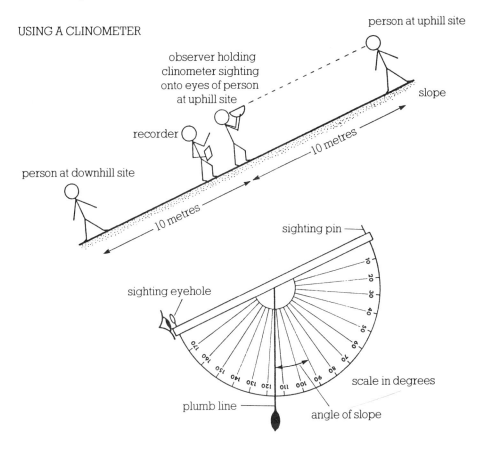

Fig 3.10 A CLINOMETER

A clinometer is really a protractor, larger than the normal size. When attached to a piece of wood, eye sights and a plumb line can be fixed to it, as shown in Fig 3.10. The angle of the slope is read as the angle between the plumb line and the central 90° line on the protractor. To use the clinometer, one assistant should stand at a convenient distance (e.g. 10 metres) uphill and another downhill from the observation point. The observer should sight the straight edge of the protractor looking into the eyes of his assistant (the assistants should be of the same height as the observer). If the plumb line is gripped against the protractor scale, the instrument may be moved and read. An average of the two readings may be found.

The second method of finding the angle of slope uses a pantometer. This is made from four pieces of wood joined as a rectangle with flexible joints. The angle is read from a protractor fixed to one of the uprights (see Fig 3.11). A spirit level indicates when the protractor upright is vertical. The instrument may simply be moved up or down the slope, giving a series of readings. It is probably more accurate than using the clinometer, can be used by one person, but is a rather large piece of equipment to carry far.

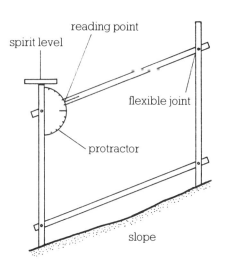

Fig 3.11 A PANTOMETER

Slope	Gradient	Steepness	Comment
35°–45°	1 in 1	Very steep	'Looks very steep'; need hands to climb
25°–35°	1 in 2 (50%)	Steep	Ascend using zigzag course; used by foresters
18°–25°	1 in 3 (33%)	Steep	Permanent grass; walking requires great effort
11°–18°	1 in 5 (20%)	Fairly steep	Limit of ploughed land; major problem for commercial road traffic
6°–11°	1 in 10 (10%)	Moderate	Walkers notice uphill climb
3°–6°	1 in 20 (5%)	Gentle	Acceptable to farmers and builders; drainage good
1°–3°	1 in 60 (1.5%)	Flat	Rather too steep for some railway operations
0.5°	—	Very flat	Below this drainage ditches are essential

Fig 3.12 SLOPE/GRADIENT TABLE

SOILS

Soils can vary considerably over quite short distances and may be linked to vegetation type, aspect and steepness of slope, and land use. In any investigation involving soils it is necessary to be able to distinguish changes in the soil. A little background reading will reveal that several recognised types of soil exist, but one rarely finds a perfect example during fieldwork.

However, it is possible to distinguish between soils, using a group of characteristics. These, when presented in a table, can enable the investigator to group the soils and provide the basis of an investigation. The characteristics are shown on the field notebook page (Fig 3.13).

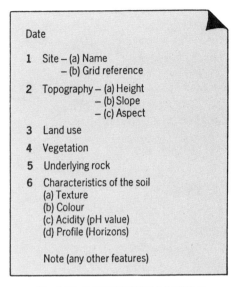

Date

1 Site – (a) Name
    – (b) Grid reference

2 Topography – (a) Height
    – (b) Slope
    – (c) Aspect

3 Land use

4 Vegetation

5 Underlying rock

6 Characteristics of the soil
(a) Texture
(b) Colour
(c) Acidity (pH value)
(d) Profile (Horizons)

Note (any other features)

Fig 3.13 A PAGE FROM A FIELD NOTEBOOK FOR RECORDING SOIL DATA

'A' horizon (surface humus layer)

'B' horizon (lighter mineral layer)

'C' horizon (pieces of rock, little humus)

underlying rock

A SOIL PROFILE

A pit dug into the soil will reveal the layers which make up what is known as the **soil profile** (see photograph). Three main layers, known as **horizons**, may be distinguished. The upper or 'A' horizon is the surface layer, dark in colour and containing plenty of rotted organic material known as 'humus'. The second or 'B' horizon contains the minerals washed down from the 'A' horizon and may be lighter in colour. Pieces of rock and only a little humus are characteristic of the 'C' horizon. Below this is the underlying rock.

Obviously one should not dig pits without permission. It may not be necessary to dig at all; soil profiles are often revealed at roadsides or in trenches dug to lay pipes or cables, or on banks of streams. A soil auger, which screws down into the soil and takes out a sample, may also be used.

The **texture** of a soil depends on the size of the rock particles it contains. It is possible to dry the soil and separate out the particles to see the proportions of different sized material it contains. A simpler method is to do this by feeling the soil in one's hands; in this way it is possible to distinguish:

1 Sandy soil – the soil is coarse, gritty to touch, with particles of sand.

2 Clayey soil – the soil is smooth and sticky when wet and easily rolled into a ball.

3 Loam – neither of the above, silky touch, only just clings to the hand.

Using this method it is possible to classify the soils into sandy – sandy loam – loam – clayey loam – clayey.

The **colour** of the soil, whilst providing another characteristic, can also give an indication of how well the soil is drained. Five groups may be distinguished:

1 Dark colour – a loose, usually shallow soil, which is extremely well drained.

2 Brown colour – a freely drained soil.

3 Brown colour/colour patches – found too around some root channels, less well drained.

4 Grey colour – colour patches around all root channels, poorly drained.

5 Peat black/pale brownish yellow patches – very poorly drained.

It is possible to make a colour chart using paint manufacturers' colour charts and some advice from a teacher.

Soil acidity	pH value	
Strongly alkaline	8.5	
Most plants suffer from alkalinity	8.0	
Mildly alkaline	7.5	Barley, Sugar beet Lucerne
Neutral	7.0	Wheat
Optimum for most plants	6.5	Red clover, Turnips Swedes
Slightly acid	6.0	Cabbage, Potatoes
Moderately acid	5.5	Kale, White clover Oats/Rye
Most plants suffer from acidity	5.0	
Extremely acid	4.5	Types of grass
	4.0	
	3.5	
	3.0	

Fig 3.14 SOIL ACIDITY TABLE

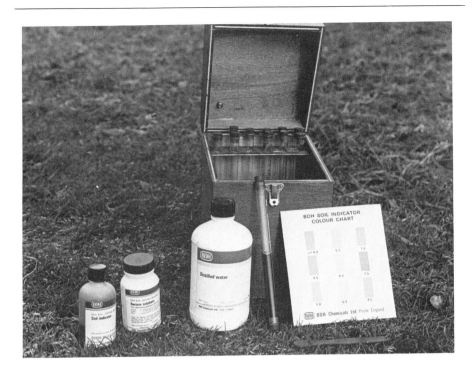

A SOIL TESTING KIT

One of the most frequently used tests on soil is that to find the acidity of the soil, i.e. to find the **pH value**. As Fig 3.14 shows, different crops require different pH values if they are to grow well. The same is true of all types of vegetation. The importance of this value is that quite small variations in the minerals in the soil can have a marked effect on the pH value.

A small soil sample is required for the test; this should be mixed in a test tube with distilled water, barium sulphate and the indicator liquid. The tube should then be shaken and left to stand until a clear coloured liquid develops. The colour of the liquid in the tube will indicate the pH value when compared with a colour scale.

• • • • • • • • • • *remember* • • • • • • • • • •

1   To record the exact location of the site where the soil is being sampled.

2   To record carefully where any sample of soil taken back to the laboratory comes from.

VEGETATION

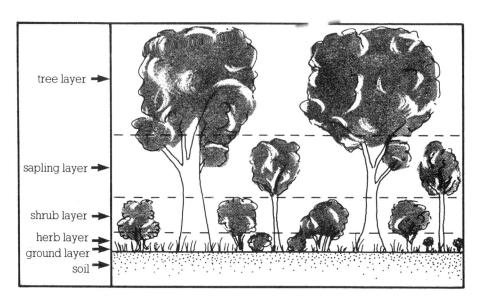

Fig 3.15 STRATIFICATION OF WOODLAND

Does the vegetation on one side of a valley differ from that on another? Does the vegetation on a north facing slope differ from that on a south facing slope? Does the vegetation on a steep slope differ from that on a gentle slope? Are differences in vegetation linked to differences in rock type or soil type? The answers to these and many other questions concerning vegetation all require a study of just what vegetation is growing in a particular area. In order to do this it is necessary to record the vegetation in an area in such a way that it can be compared with that in another area.

One way of doing this is to record the layers or stratification of vegetation in an area (see Fig 3.15). Plants grow to different levels, each occupying its own level, and they often flower and fruit at different times in order to survive. To undertake the survey it is necessary to measure the heights of the plants growing at the site. Obviously this is an enormous task, so it is sensible to take an area (e.g. 500 square metres) as a sample. The heights of smaller shrubs and plants may be measured with a tape measure. Taller trees may prove more difficult. They may be measured by using a clinometer to find one angle of the right angled triangle, and then measuring the distance from the tree, to give the figures necessary to work out the height (see Fig 3.16). Alternatively a hypsometer may be used (see Fig 3.17).

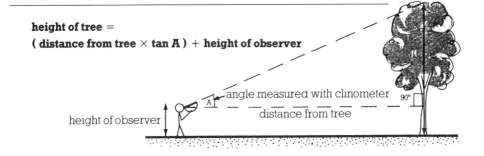

height of tree =
(distance from tree × tan A) + height of observer

angle measured with clinometer

height of observer

distance from tree

Fig 3.16 TO FIND THE HEIGHT OF A TREE

The spread of plants – that is the ground area they cover – may be worked out by measuring the distance from the centre to the outer edge at each of the eight points of the compass. The average radial distance (r) may then be used to work out the approximate area of spread (area = πr^2).

The frequency with which plants of different species occur within the herb layer presents a difficult problem. Because there are so many plants a sample survey method is needed to find which are the most frequently occurring species. One could throw a hoop, either at random points or following a transect in an area, and record the species it covers.

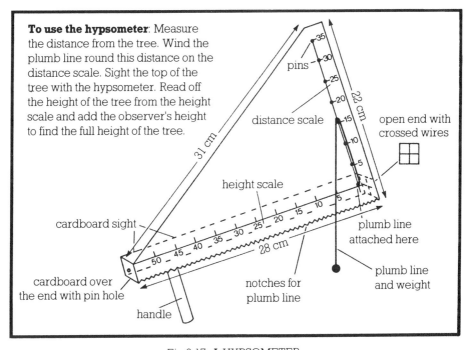

To use the hypsometer: Measure the distance from the tree. Wind the plumb line round this distance on the distance scale. Sight the top of the tree with the hypsometer. Read off the height of the tree from the height scale and add the observer's height to find the full height of the tree.

Fig 3.17 A HYPSOMETER

knitting needle
sample at intersection of strings

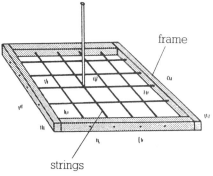

frame

strings

Fig 3.18 THE QUADRAT SURVEY
TECHNIQUE

Alternatively, quadrats may be used. These are square frames which are divided into a smaller grid of squares with strong string. Obviously the frame needs to be larger than the plants in the area being sampled. A standard size is a one metre square frame using string tied at 20 cm intervals along each side of it (see Fig 3.18). The quadrat is placed on the ground at random points and a long knitting needle dropped from each grid intersection: the species this needle touches is recorded.

From this information the frequency of a species within each quadrat may be recorded (e.g. 4 hits out of 16 would be 25%). This will reveal any differences between parts of the area being studied. The frequency of a species in the area may be found by finding the chance of making at least one 'hit' on the species in a quadrat. If the species is found in 38 quadrats out of 100, then the frequency is 38%.

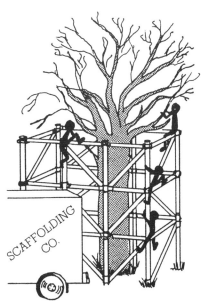

Measuring tree height: taller trees may prove more difficult!

1 Join with a neighbour and discuss ways of presenting the data discovered during (a) a survey of stratification, and (b) a survey of vegetation frequency on a hillside.

2 Draw out a table which could be used for recording in a field notebook the information collected during a vegetation frequency survey.

RIVERS AND STREAMS

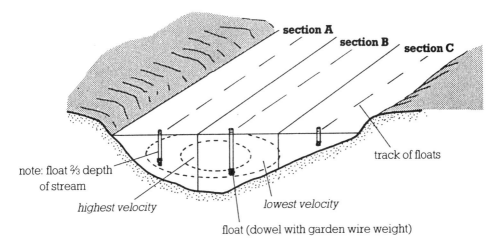

Fig 3.19 HOW TO MEASURE VELOCITY

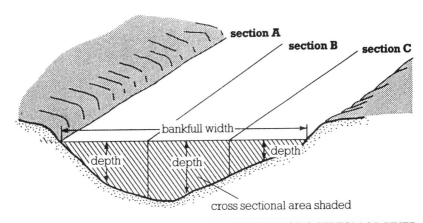

Fig 3.20 HOW TO FIND THE AREA OF THE CROSS SECTION OF A STREAM OR RIVER

The amount of water flowing down a river or stream, known as the **discharge**, is of concern to many people. In times of drought and in times of flood people living nearby may be affected. Measuring the discharge of a river or stream can form the basis of various studies. The discharge may be found by multiplying the velocity (that is the speed of flow of the water) by the area of the cross section of the stream (see next page).

It is possible to find the **velocity** of a stream very accurately using a current meter. This consists of a propeller which is placed in the water and is linked to a control box from which readings may be taken. Although it may be possible to make this equipment, it is difficult to use in deep water.

An alternative is to use floats. However, floats on the surface of the water may give inaccurate readings as the velocity of a stream is less at the sides and surface than in the centre (see Fig 3.19). Wind over the surface may also affect the result. The best method therefore is to have floats of different lengths to measure the velocity in different parts of the stream. The floats made of thin dowel, can be weighted by winding garden wire round one end, so that they float upright with their tips just breaking the surface. The stream may be divided into sections (see Fig 3.19) and the float used to measure the velocity in each section should be approximately two thirds the depth of the stream. The floats should be floated at least 10 times in each section over a measured 10 metre track. The track should be at least one third of a metre deep and clear of obstructions and as straight as possible. Work out the mean (average) time of the 10 runs to find the velocity of the water in that section. The velocity in metres per second for each section is the distance (10 m) divided by the average time (secs).

In order to discover the discharge, however, it is necessary to find the **cross sectional area** of the water in the stream or river. This may be done using a weir with a 'V' notch cut into it which gives an easily identified section. These are not easy to construct and the water authority should be consulted before an attempt at construction is made. However, the area can be found by measuring the bankfull width of the stream (see Fig 3.20) and the depth, using string marked in metres and/or 10 cm intervals with nail varnish and weighted at one end. The area of each section for which the velocity was measured may be found by multiplying the width of the section by the depth.

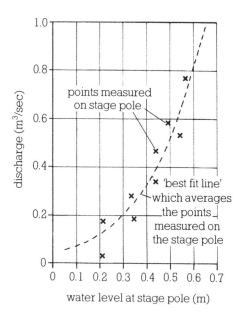

Fig 3.21 A RATING CURVE

By multiplying the area of the section by its velocity the discharge may be calculated:

$$\text{discharge (m}^3\text{/sec)} = \text{velocity (m/sec)} \times \text{area (m}^2\text{)}$$

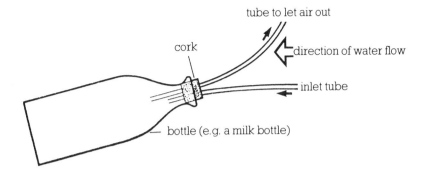

tube to let air out

cork

direction of water flow

inlet tube

bottle (e.g. a milk bottle)

Fig 3.22 A SEDIMENT SAMPLER

Adding the results for each section together will give the discharge of the whole stream. The same technique can be used when calculating the discharge of a large river. In this case it may not be feasible to use floats, but on a calm day a brightly coloured object (e.g. an orange) may be floated down a measured 10 metre track. To compensate for the fact that only surface speed is being measured the result should be multiplied by 0.8. A bridge can be used to measure width and depth.

To test ideas involving the use of these techniques it is often necessary to monitor discharge at regular intervals over a period of time. One way of avoiding the need to measure velocity each time is to set up a permanent stage pole in the stream. This large pole should be graduated in centimetres over the expected depth of river levels. Once discharge has been measured on a number of occasions the results could be graphed and a 'rating curve' produced, allowing discharge to be estimated by reading the depths on the stage pole (see Fig 3.21).

Several ideas may be tested using these methods, for instance the relationship between discharge and rainfall, or the relationship between the discharge of several streams and the size of their drainage basins.

All rivers and streams carry material down with them. This material is known as **load** and may be investigated through fieldwork. The load is carried in three basic ways: in solution, when it is dissolved in the water; in suspension, when it is visible and carried in the water (for instance, the mud seen in a river in flood); and as bedload, the rocks trundled along the bottom of the stream or river. Load in solution and suspension may be compared with discharge. Bedload may be investigated in pools (deeper areas of a stream) and in riffles (the shallower sections) to study differences in shape and size.

A sample of the **solution load** may be acquired by taking a sample of the water in a clean bottle. The sample then needs to be filtered to take out the load carried in suspension. Once filtered, the sample can be evaporated to dryness, the residue being the soluble load. Some analysis of the sample may be possible with the help of the Chemistry Department, but often quite large samples of water are required.

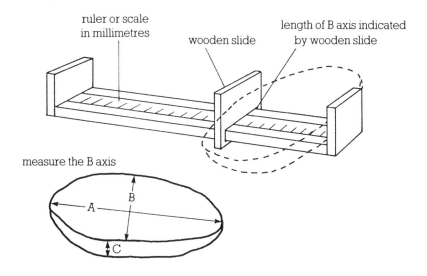

Fig 3.23 MEASURING PEBBLES

Suspended sediment should be collected from the stream using a sediment sampler. This is easy to make (see Fig 3.22), and because the suspended sediment distribution varies with depth, the sampler should be moved up and down in the water until full. The sample should be taken upstream of the person operating the sampler, which can be fixed to a rod if the water is deep. If the sample is filtered after shaking the bottle in the laboratory, the suspended load will be left on the filter paper. It is possible to weigh the sediment by weighing the filter paper before filtering, then weighing the *dry* filter paper and sediment after filtering, the difference in weights being the weight of the sediment. Suspended sediment is usually given as parts per million (p.p.m.) and may be worked out using this formula:

$$\text{suspended sediment (p.p.m.)} = \frac{\text{weight of sediment(g)} \times 10^6}{\text{volume of water sample (cm}^3)}$$

However, it may be simpler to build up a graph of the weight of sediment against velocity and discharge to test whether these have any effect on the amount of suspended sediment carried.

Larger material is involved when the **bedload** is measured. This consists of stones and pebbles of a variety of sizes which are lying on the bed of the stream. One problem which arises immediately is how to choose a sample (see pages 17–18). The most straightforward approach is to use a random sample by wading into the stream and at each pace picking up the pebble nearest the toes of the collector's boots. This should be done regardless of size of the pebble or a misrepresentation will occur if only hand sized pebbles are collected. The stones should be measured across the B axis (which gives the most reliable measure of size) using a pebbleometer (see Fig 3.23). A sample of 50 pebbles at each site would be a suitable number. By recording the size of each pebble, graphs of the results may be drawn.

---

1 Make a list of (a) the equipment you would need, and (b) the steps you would take to discover the discharge of a stream.

2 Draw out a table, as on a page of a field notebook, for recording the results of the float speeds along a stream.

3 Use Fig 3.21, 'A rating curve', to estimate the discharge at the following depths on the stage pole (a) 0.3 metres (b) 0.6 metres.

4 List the steps you would take to make either a sediment sampler or a pebbleometer.

THE SEA AND THE SHORE

Beach materials vary in size with distance from the sea, angle of slope of the beach and height. Slope angles on beaches/dunes differ according to the amount of vegetation growing on them. Wave characteristics vary depending on the strength and direction of the wind. These and many other statements may be tested on the coast and can provide the basis for investigations on the sea-shore. The coast is an area where people often attempt to interfere with natural processes. They build groynes and sea walls and use bulldozers to change the shape of a beach (for instance, by building up shingle banks to protect the area behind them). The effects of such activities may also provide the basis for a study over time or for a comparison study.

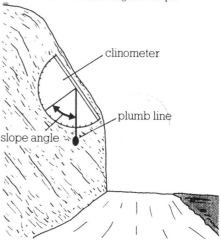

clinometer held at a distance from the cliff to measure angle of slope

clinometer

plumb line

slope angle

Fig 3.24 MEASURING CLIFF ANGLE

The general shape of cliffs may be investigated in terms of height, angle and composition. The height of a cliff may be calculated by using the same method as that for finding the height of trees (see page 46). Angle may be calculated by using a clinometer – stand away from the cliff and to one side and hold the straight edge parallel to the slope of the cliff (see Fig 3.24). The angle may vary at different heights and the point at which the angle varies could be measured. Finding out the composition of the cliff will require a look at a geological map or the collection and identification of specimens.

WARNING

Be careful, cliffs can be dangerous – do not climb – collect specimens from material at the bottom of the cliff. Do not dig them from the cliff itself.

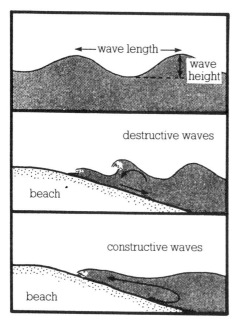

wave length

wave height

destructive waves

beach

constructive waves

beach

Fig 3.25 WAVES

Types of waves have a direct bearing on the type of shoreline. They may be constructive or destructive. Constructive waves tend to have greater wave length and be less steep than destructive waves (see Fig 3.25). Measurements of wave height are possible against a tide board of a pier or chalk marks placed at low tide on a leg of a pier. The wave length may be measured in terms of the period between successive wave crests. Count the number of waves breaking or passing a point each minute for a time span of approximately 10 minutes and find the mean total per minute. Wave frequencies of below 13 per minute are considered constructive and those above 13 per minute destructive.

Waves break on the beach and run up the beach as swash, then flow back again as backwash. Some of the water which arrives on the beach with the swash will soak into the beach material and return to the sea through the beach particles. This water does no work in moving beach material. The more water returning in the backwash, the more material is likely to be moved by that water. The different depths of swash and backwash may be measured by driving a graduated stick into the beach in the run-up zone. It would be interesting to see whether this varies as the tide comes in or goes out and with the changes in beach material and slope it may cross.

Date ....

Location ....

State of tide (rising/falling) ....

Wind direction ....

Wind force ....

READING	Frequency (No.of waves per min)	Wave height	Wave length	Wave steepness Height ÷ length	Length of run-up	Depth of swash	Depth of backwash
1							
2							
3							
4							
5							
6							
7							
8							
9							
10							
Mean							

Fig 3.26 A PAGE FROM A FIELD NOTEBOOK FOR RECORDING WAVE DATA

ON THE BEACH

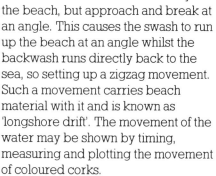

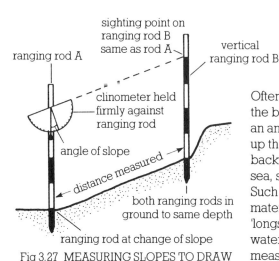

sighting point on
ranging rod B
same as rod A

ranging rod A

vertical
ranging rod B

clinometer held
firmly against
ranging rod

angle of slope

distance measured

both ranging rods in
ground to same depth

ranging rod at change of slope

Fig 3.27 MEASURING SLOPES TO DRAW
A PROFILE

Often waves do not break directly onto the beach, but approach and break at an angle. This causes the swash to run up the beach at an angle whilst the backwash runs directly back to the sea, so setting up a zigzag movement. Such a movement carries beach material with it and is known as 'longshore drift'. The movement of the water may be shown by timing, measuring and plotting the movement of coloured corks.

Painted pebbles may be used to indicate the movement of beach material. Pebbles placed in a line at right angles to the sea at low tide may be collected at the next low tide and their movement plotted. The paint does need to be bright and particularly hard wearing, or it will be washed off by the action of the sea. Quite a large number of pebbles will be required, as many will be lost. It is possible to measure the movement of material of different sizes, although marking very fine material presents difficulties (dyes may be used).

Beaches are not all flat; they rise away from the sea and many have several different levels. Indeed, shingle beaches contain banks of material which may be used for study. To find the shape of the beach, a beach profile may be constructed. This involves plotting the distance between different changes in level to discover the length and angle of different slopes. Ranging rods, which are poles painted with red and white sections of equal length, are placed on the beach at the breaks in slope. The distance between them is measured and a clinometer used to find the angle of slope (see Fig 3.27). From this data a profile may be drawn.

Sea Beet

It may be rewarding to measure the size of beach material at each level on the profile. Using a 30 cm quadrat placed randomly at each level, the pebbles on the surface within the quadrat may be counted and measured. It is useful to mark each pebble with felt pen when counting and before measuring, to avoid confusion. Measuring may be carried out using the same technique as for stones in a stream (see page 51). In addition, you could record how angular or rounded the pebble is (see Fig 3.28). Such studies are best carried out at several points on the beach and results compared with the direction of longshore drift.

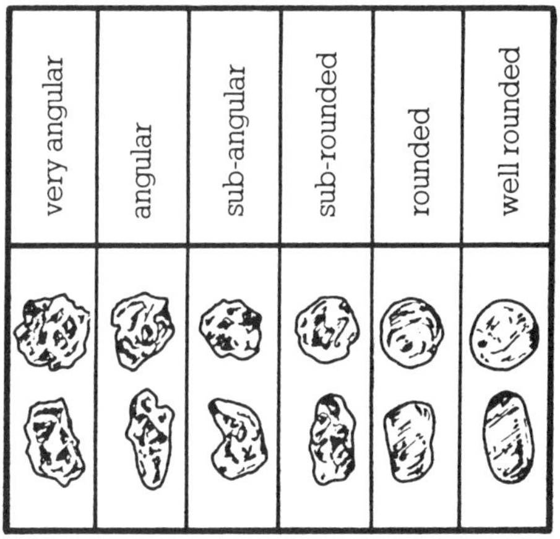

Fig 3.28 ROUNDNESS INDEX CHART

As the beach material becomes stable it may be colonised by a variety of plants which are adapted to growing in coastal conditions. Behind the banks of beach deposits plants may grow on salt marshes. Such plants are often readily identified and play an important part in stabilising the coast: indeed grasses are often planted by people to stabilise sand dunes. The vegetation may be sampled using a transect and/or a quadrat (see page 47). The results may be viewed in connection with work on the profile of the beach and on size of beach material.

Other plants commonly found in coastal areas: Sea Plantain
Shrubby Seablite
Sea Aster
Sea Lavender
Marsh Samphire

Sea Purslane

Common Seablite

Fig 3.29 PLANTS COMMONLY FOUND IN COASTAL AREAS

1 Draw out a notebook page suitable for recording the data required for drawing the profile of a beach, and for recording data collected on beach materials.

2 Draw sketches like those to the left of three of the five other plants which are often found on beaches or in saltmarsh areas.

COUNTING PEOPLE

Geographers are interested in people. Not only are they interested in the number of people in a place, but in the density (how crowded an area is); the distribution (where the people are); and in the people themselves, their ages, what work they do, and their patterns of movement.

Much of the information about people in an area is obtained from the census. The first census in Britain was held in 1801, and one has been held every ten years since then (except in 1941 due to the War). Details about the census material may be found on page 134. It is possible to find population information before 1801 from books in which historians have found material which enables them to estimate the population of a place, and from parish registers.

Work from parish registers is, however, not easy and it is probably essential to discuss the possibilities with someone who can give good advice. The registers can be used to tabulate totals of monthly births and deaths and gain an idea into the causes of sudden fluctuations. An increase in burials during the summer months could well be the result of a plague, and a winter peak in burials or one in early spring could be the result of a famine.

Total population figures for a place can show how the population has changed over a period of time. A line graph, labelled with the major events in the history of the place (such as the building of the railway or a large industrial complex) helps to begin to outline the causes for any changes in population.

Geographers have suggested that the distribution of people in a large town or city has changed. They point out that before people had easy access to transport, towns were small and very densely populated, particularly near the centre. As transport became more widely available the pattern changed; they were still more densely populated near the centre but there were large areas of low density on the outskirts. Recently these areas, the suburbs, have become more densely populated whilst the central areas have lost population.

This pattern could be investigated for any large town or city, using census material which gives details of population in the various wards (see page 134) in the town. It would then be possible to find out why these changes have occurred, from books and from the Local Collection (see page 133). You could also look at how changes have affected the lives of people who have lived for a long time in areas where change has been greatest.

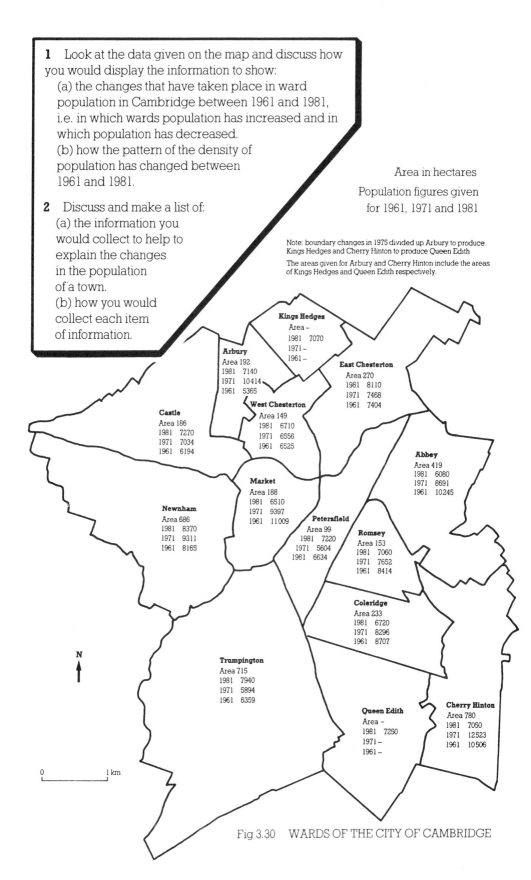

1 Look at the data given on the map and discuss how you would display the information to show:
    (a) the changes that have taken place in ward population in Cambridge between 1961 and 1981, i.e. in which wards population has increased and in which population has decreased.
    (b) how the pattern of the density of population has changed between 1961 and 1981.

2 Discuss and make a list of:
    (a) the information you would collect to help to explain the changes in the population of a town.
    (b) how you would collect each item of information.

Area in hectares
Population figures given
for 1961, 1971 and 1981

Note: boundary changes in 1975 divided up Arbury to produce Kings Hedges and Cherry Hinton to produce Queen Edith

The areas given for Arbury and Cherry Hinton include the areas of Kings Hedges and Queen Edith respectively.

Kings Hedges
Area –
1981 7070
1971 –
1961 –

Arbury
Area 192
1981 7140
1971 10414
1961 5365

East Chesterton
Area 270
1981 8110
1971 7468
1961 7404

West Chesterton
Area 149
1981 6710
1971 6556
1961 6525

Castle
Area 186
1981 7270
1971 7034
1961 6194

Abbey
Area 419
1981 6080
1971 8691
1961 10245

Market
Area 188
1981 6510
1971 9397
1961 11009

Newnham
Area 686
1981 8370
1971 9311
1961 8165

Petersfield
Area 99
1981 7220
1971 5604
1961 6634

Romsey
Area 153
1981 7060
1971 7652
1961 8414

Coleridge
Area 233
1981 6720
1971 8296
1961 8707

N

Trumpington
Area 715
1981 7940
1971 5894
1961 6359

Queen Edith
Area –
1981 7250
1971 –
1961 –

Cherry Hinton
Area 780
1981 7050
1971 12523
1961 10506

0   1 km

Fig 3.30 WARDS OF THE CITY OF CAMBRIDGE

MORE PEOPLE

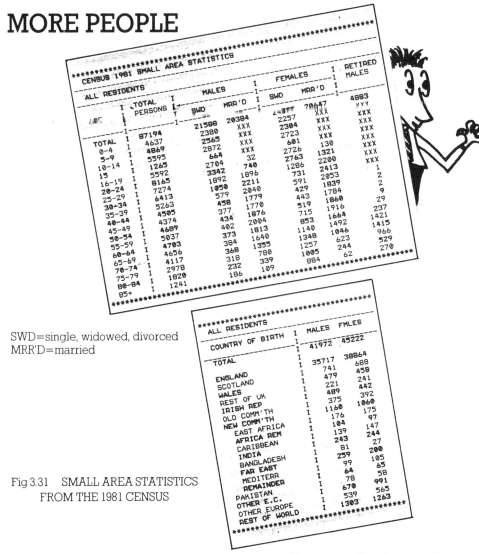

SWD=single, widowed, divorced
MRR'D=married

Fig 3.31   SMALL AREA STATISTICS
FROM THE 1981 CENSUS

Population changes have occurred in villages as well as in towns. It has been noticed that large villages with easy access to a town or city have increased in population between 1931 and 1981. By contrast, population has decreased in smaller isolated villages further away from a town or city.

This idea may be tested using census data. The population of parishes, which contain a village and include surrounding hamlets and farms, may be listed for 1931 and 1981. A percentage increase or decrease may then be calculated using the formula:

$$\% \text{ increase/decrease} = \frac{\text{population for } 1981 \times 100}{\text{population for } 1931}$$

The distance from a large town or city may be measured using a map of the area being studied. To find which villages have easy access, the distance from the town by main road could be calculated.

---

1 The idea given in the first paragraph may be divided into three ideas to test:

(i) The population of large villages has increased, whilst the population of small villages has decreased, between 1931 and 1981.

(ii) Large villages which have increased in population are near to the city, whilst small villages whose population has decreased between 1931 and 1981 are further away.

(iii) Large villages which have increased in population and are further from the city have easy access to the city, whilst the small villages with a declining population are more isolated.

   (a) What decisions concerning which villages to choose need to be taken before this project can be tackled?

   (b) How would you use the formula giving percentage increase/decrease to test idea (i)?

   (c) Explain how you would test ideas (ii) and (iii), assuming that you have found the information relating to distance from the major town or city.

The changes in population in villages can have a real effect on the number of services offered to the people who live there. Kelly's Directory (see page 133) could be used to find the services offered in 1931. Field survey work is probably the only way to discover the services offered in 1981, unless one wishes to look through the local telephone directory – a possible but rather long, boring job. New services such as a new motorway or road improvement scheme may affect population.

Not only are there changes in total populations, but the people change as time passes. On the next page are two graphs, known as population pyramids, showing the age and sex of the inhabitants of the same small area (enumeration district) of a housing estate on the outskirts of Cambridge.

Indeed, it is in looking at small areas that some of the most interesting information is to be found. Census material relating to individual people is not available until 100 years have passed, so you can only look at that up to 1881. From this material, information for individual streets, and homes in those streets, can

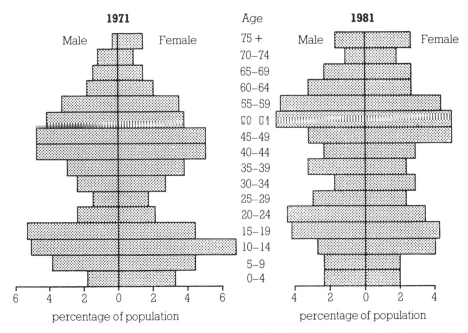

	1971		Age		1981	

Fig 3.32   AGE – SEX STRUCTURE FOR PART OF THE ARBURY ESTATE, CAMBRIDGE

be discovered. For an individual house it is possible to find the names of persons living there, the relationship of each member of the household, their age, occupation and birthplace.

Detailed information such as this could form the basis of a study of the changes which have taken place in size of household, number of children, age structure, pattern of employment, and migration trends. As such detailed data is not available for years after 1881, it would be necessary to sample the earlier data and compare it with present day information.

Again, it is important to get good advice before embarking on such a study. Census data before 1841 is rather unreliable, so it is best to use material between 1841 and 1881. Advice from historians may be particularly useful. A study of this type may be rewarding for someone who is interested in the changes that have taken place in the area in which they live.

> **2**   (a) What changes do the pyramids show have taken place in the Arbury district of Cambridge between 1971 and 1981?
> (b) What effect may such changes have on the schools in the area?

THE VILLAGE

There is one great danger in conducting a study of one particular village. That is that the study will simply be a collection of all one can find out about the village, rather than having a definite purpose. Therefore it is vitally important that the ideas that are being tested or the questions that are being asked are clear before work on data collection begins (see page 9). This will help to ensure that the study does not contain irrelevant material.

At first, it may be necessary to ask why the village is located where it is, and how far this location has affected its growth. When studying location one should take into consideration the site and position of a settlement.

The **site** refers to the nature of the land on which the settlement is built and the following provides a checklist of features to consider:
(a)   The relief of the site, including the height above sea level, the surrounding features (i.e. is the village in a valley, on a hill, on a valley side? etc.) and any changes in slope.
(b)   Aspect (see page 39) – including whether the site is sheltered or exposed.
(c)   Water supply – was there a readily available water supply when the settlement was first established?
(d)   Geology – is the rock on which the village is built particularly solid or different from the surrounding area?
– was or is the rock where the village is built of particular economic value?

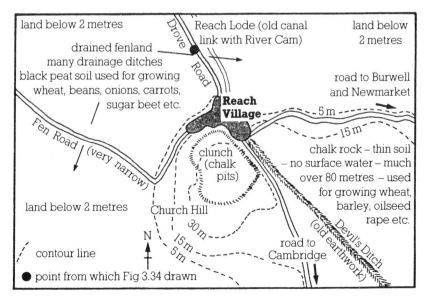

Fig 3.33   SKETCH MAP OF THE SITE AND POSITION OF REACH

(e) Soils – is the site on or near soils of value to farmers?

(f) Is there a particular peculiarity of the site which makes it attractive, e.g. at the crossing point of a river, at the head of a sea inlet, etc?

In working through these features it is worth noting particular advantages of the site (it may be, for instance, a particularly good defensive site or by a source of power) and particular disadvantages of the site (a lack of room for expansion, for example).

Although it may be possible to gain some ideas from an Ordnance Survey map, field observation is essential if this is to be completed properly.

The **position** of a settlement is its location in relation to the settlements, communications and area around it. A checklist of features to consider might consist of:

(a) The physical setting – is there a variety of types of land nearby which the villagers may use or have used in the past?

(b) Transport routes – what types of transport serve the village?; what is their condition (for instance, are they disused?); what is their status? (are the roads main or minor roads?); do they terminate at the settlement?

(c) Distance to neighbouring settlements and towns – it may be useful to look at local public transport services: often time taken is more important than distance. As new roads are built, and bus services withdrawn, the situation regarding position may change, and it is useful to be aware of changes which have taken place.

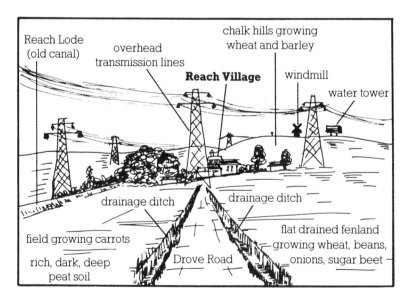

Fig 3.34   SKETCH TO SHOW THE SITE AND POSITION OF REACH
(LOOKING SSE FROM FEN DROVE)

> **1** Look at the map (Fig 3.33) and sketch (Fig 3.34) illustrating the site and position of Reach.
> (a) Use the information to make a list of the main features of site and the main features of position.
> (b) Is the map or the sketch more useful in illustrating the site and position of the village, or do they complement each other? Give reasons for your answer.
> **2** Write out two questions or ideas to test which would involve the use of information regarding site and position.

THE VILLAGE GROWS AND CHANGES

A village may grow in terms of population (see page 57), or in terms of areal size (which is the concern of this section). There are several aspects of growth which may be investigated. They include:
(a)   The area covered by development at a particular time, i.e. the rate of growth.
(b)   The direction(s) in which that growth occurred.
(c)   The time at which the growth took place.
(d)   The form which the growth took, i.e. the type of building – whether industrial, public buildings or residential; and the pattern of growth, i.e. the design of the buildings and the layout of the area.

Similarly, there are several aspects of change which may be investigated, for instance:
(a)   The changes in function of the village, i.e. its main activity – it may have changed from being a farming village to being an industrial or dormitory village.
(b)   The changes in the style of building and housing which have taken place and in building material used.
(c)   The changes in the services offered in the village – the shops, bus services, recreation and schooling facilities.
(d)   The changes in the type of people who live in the village, e.g. their ages and their types and places of work.

Much of this information relating to growth and change may be collected on a base map of the village. A scale of 1:1250 is probably the easiest to work with, although maps of other scales could be used.

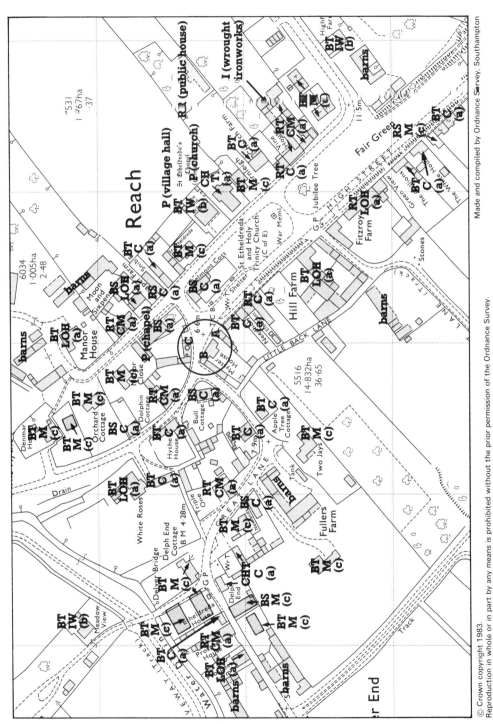

SURVEY OF REACH VILLAGE (RECORDED ON 1:2500 ORDNANCE SURVEY MAPS TL 5666 and TL 5766) SEE TEXT FOR KEY

© Crown copyright 1983.
Reproduction in whole or in part by any means is prohibited without the prior permission of the Ordnance Survey.

Made and compiled by Ordnance Survey, Southampton

There are four features for each building which need to be collected to obtain much of the information for all except (d) in the previous list. The four are:

(i)   Function – i.e. what the building is used for. In a village only those buildings which are non-residential need to be recorded, for example:

P   public building (with its actual function written next to it) e.g. school
S   shop (the type of shop could be written next to the symbol) e.g. post office
I   industry (the type of industry could be written next to the symbol) e.g. wroughtironworks
F   agricultural – farms or farm buildings
RR   recreational (the type of facility could be written next to the symbol) e.g. public house, village hall

(ii)   Building material – a list of possible building materials can be noted down by quickly looking at the village during a preliminary survey. In Reach they would be:

Walls   **B**   Brick
　　　　CH   Chalk (the local name is 'clunch')
　　　　R   Rendering (a covering over the original material)
Roofs   **T**   Tile
　　　　TH   Thatch
　　　　S   Slate

(iii)   Style of building – this need only be completed for residential buildings and refers to the design of the buildings. In a village it may be necessary to develop a list of types for that village, rather than using the type of lists used for towns (see page 69). An example of such a list may be:

C   old cottage (pre 1900)
CM   old cottage (pre 1900), extensive external modernisation
LOH   large old house (pre 1900)
IW   house built between 1900 and 1945
M   modern house (post 1945)

An example of each of these should be sketched and labelled.

(iv)   Age of building – it is best to think in terms of broad bands of age, for example:
(a) pre 1900
(b) 1900–1945
(c) post 1945

It may be possible to be more exact in some cases as dates may appear on houses or may be discovered from other sources: this will give a more accurate pattern of growth. But inhabitants should not be disturbed and asked the age of their house.

MODERNISED COTTAGE   INTER WAR HOUSE

In each of the lists there are letters
which provide a key to the field map of
Reach on page 65. Notice that the key
symbols are easy to remember and
are all different, so that they can be
easily distinguished when the data is
presented.

MODERN HOUSE

Historical sources or small booklets about the history of the village
may add to this information, as may old maps. But they should only be
used to provide background information; they should not be allowed
to dominate the study. Information about changes in services may be
obtained from historical sources (see page 133).

Investigations into the changes in the ages and occupations of the
inhabitants of the village, and their links with places outside the
village, will involve the use of census material (see page 59 for
population and age structure) and questionnaires (see page 19).

PART OF REACH VILLAGE (AREA CIRCLED ON MAP)

Questionnaires could be used to develop the idea that there have been changes in where people work, from mainly in the village to mainly in nearby towns. They may also be used for investigations into the movements of villagers, e.g. for shopping and entertainment. However, the advice about the use of questionnaires (page 19) should be read carefully first.

1 The photograph of Reach contains two housing styles which are not shown in the photographs opposite. Draw labelled sketches of these two styles and name them from list (iii).
2 The survey of the buildings shown in the photograph has not been included on the map (page 65) – the section of the map is circled. Use the photograph to give the labels for buildings **A**, **B** and **C**.
3 Discuss with your neighbour:
(a) possible ideas which could be tested using the map on page 65.
(b) how the information could be presented (see pages 119–21).
(c) what the map shows of the growth and changes in the village of Reach.

PATTERNS IN TOWNS
GROWTH

Has the town grown outwards equally on all sides (i.e. in concentric rings) from the centre? Or has there been more growth at particular times in certain directions? What were the main building types and styles used at different periods during this growth? Are all the areas equally pleasant places in which to live? These and many other questions could provide the starting point for a study of town growth.

Maps from the town library or from another source (see page 25) would provide background information on the growth of the town. But a study of the effect of that pattern of growth, particularly on the residential areas of the town, will involve fieldwork.

As in the case of the village (see page 64), the age and style of building will provide evidence of the type of growth which took place at various periods. The style of building is also one part of what makes up the 'character' of a town.

There are many architectural styles which can be recognised in towns and a decision will need to be taken on how detailed the study is to be. Fig 3.35 illustrates how the detailed list A can be reduced to the relatively short list C. Not all styles will necessarily be found in a town. In some towns certain styles will predominate.

LIST A		LIST B	LIST C
Medieval	before 1485	Early	
Tudor	1485–1600		
Jacobean	1600–1649		
Carolean	1649–1688	Stuart	Pre Victorian
Queen Anne	1689–1714		
Early Georgian	1714–1760	Georgian	
Late Georgian	1760–1811		
Regency	1811–1837	Regency	
Victorian	1837–1901	Victorian	Victorian/Edwardian
Edwardian	1901–1918	Edwardian	
Inter War	1919–1939	Inter War	Inter War
Post War	after 1945	Post War	Post War

Fig 3.35   BUILDING STYLES

TUDOR

GEORGIAN

VICTORIAN TERRACE

INTER WAR

POST WAR 1960s

PRESENT DAY

As with any overview of style, there are great variations within each category. For example, in the Victorian period, types range from the large individual 'villa' for the wealthy to the terraced rows for the workers. However, in most towns the types of housing covering the greatest area will be those built during the Victorian (1837–1901), the inter war (1919–1939) and the post war (after 1945) periods.

If work surveying building style is to be undertaken, then it is necessary to learn how to distinguish different styles. A look round the town beforehand will give some idea of the styles to be encountered, and will help to decide on the detail required. Whatever is decided, it is advisable to include a sketch in a field notebook of a typical house for each style recorded.

LAND USE

Residential
P1 Small, terraced, pre World War 1 housing
P2 Larger, terraced or semi-detached, pre World War 1 housing
P3 Large, pre World War 1 houses, set in their own grounds
IW Detached and semi-detached inter war houses and bungalows with gardens
M1 Modern council housing
M2 Modern, privately owned housing of small or medium size
M3 Modern, large detached or semi-detached houses
F(H) Flats (**FH** – high rise)

Industry
I – letter **I** used to indicate all types of industry

Commercial
S Shops
O Offices
B Banks
W Warehouses

Public buildings
P – name the buildings, e.g. schools, churches, council buildings etc.

Open space
FA Farmland
R Recreational – name type, e.g. allotments, park, swimming pool etc.
CE Cemetery
D(R) Derelict or wasteland (**DR** – derelict land in process of redevelopment)

Resort functions
BH Boarding houses
H Hotels

Entertainment
E Entertainment – cinemas, arcades etc.

Transport
T – name the use, e.g. railway, car park, airport etc.

Fig 3.36 URBAN LAND USE SURVEY – CHECKLIST FOR RECORDING INFORMATION

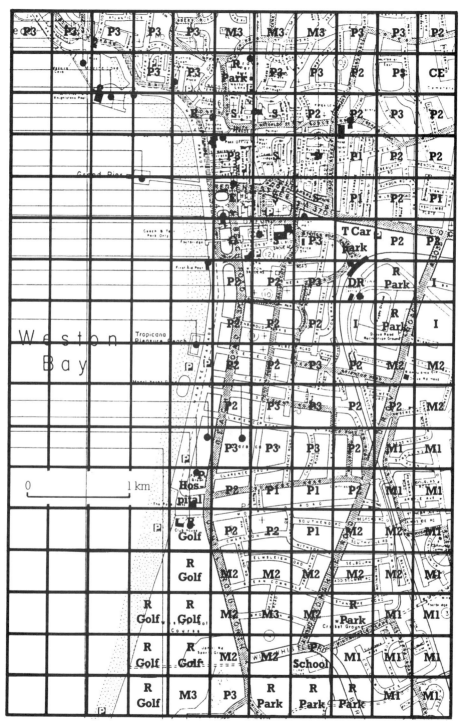

LAND USE OF PART OF WESTON-SUPER-MARE RECORDED ON A TOWN MAP
(SEE OPPOSITE FOR KEY)

The way in which land is used in towns is a major concern of geographers. A survey of land use will raise other questions as to why the land is used in particular ways. Some idea of this may be gained by comparing land use with other factors, such as distance from the city centre, distance from main transport routes, and the availability of land.

A checklist of types of land use found in towns, with possible key letters, is shown on page 71 (Fig 3.36). If the town being studied has a particular function – in Weston-Super-Mare (see map on page 72) it is a resort function – then an additional category could be added.

A major problem when collecting data for urban studies relating to growth and land use is the size of the task. It would be a long and unnecessary job to plot each individual house. Indeed, in large cities it would be almost impossible.

One method which could be used in a small town was shown on the previous page. A map of the town, in this case Weston-Super-Mare, is divided into a series of squares. The smaller the squares the more detailed the study and the more accurate it will be. As with sampling it is necessary to choose a balance between accuracy and the time available. A preliminary survey will help. In this case a street map (obtained from the Weston-Super-Mare Tourist Information Centre) has been used as a base map. The letters in the urban land use survey checklist have acted as a key. The letter in each square is the main or dominant ground floor land use in that square. A different use may be found on different floors of taller buildings and this is reviewed later (see pages 76–7). This data may then be used as the basis for a map of land use.

1 What type of building does the map on page 72 show is to be found:
  (a) in the northern part of Weston-Super-Mare?
  (b) in the south eastern part of Weston-Super-Mare?
  (c) around the central shopping area of Weston-Super-Mare?

2 What evidence does this map give of the pattern of land use and growth of Weston-Super-Mare?

PATTERNS IN CITIES

Point 42 is right here!

To record details of buildings and land use in large cities either some form of sampling is required or the study will need to be restricted to a small specific area of the city.

One method of sampling is to record data at certain points over the whole city area. These points may be chosen at random or at measured regular intervals (see pages 17–18). The main building type or land use needs to be recorded on a recording sheet. Once the data has been collected, it can be transferred to a base map – accurate recording of each location is therefore important. Lines may then be drawn round areas with a similar main building or land use type.

There are difficulties with this type of collection. It requires a great deal of travelling around the city. Also, unless quite a large number of points are chosen, it is difficult to draw lines round areas with any degree of certainty.

Another method of sampling which may provide a more satisfactory answer is that of a line sample (transect). This involves choosing one or more lines across an area or a city and noting the data required on each side of this line. Roads which take a direct route across the city may be followed.

A map is not essential to collect data in this way. Fig 3.37 shows the results of such a survey. The recorder draws two vertical lines on the recording sheet and, starting at the bottom, records the land use types. The scale is decided by the number of paces before the type changes. In this way different types of data may be collected and changes noted across the city.

Using this technique studies may be undertaken, such as those based on the idea that the function (the use of) buildings, the type of land use, age and height of building vary with distance from the centre in a similar way in every direction.

Great detail may be included on such recording sheets, but it is important to remember only to collect data relevant to the study being undertaken: to collect any more is unnecessary and time consuming. However, it is important to be as accurate as possible.

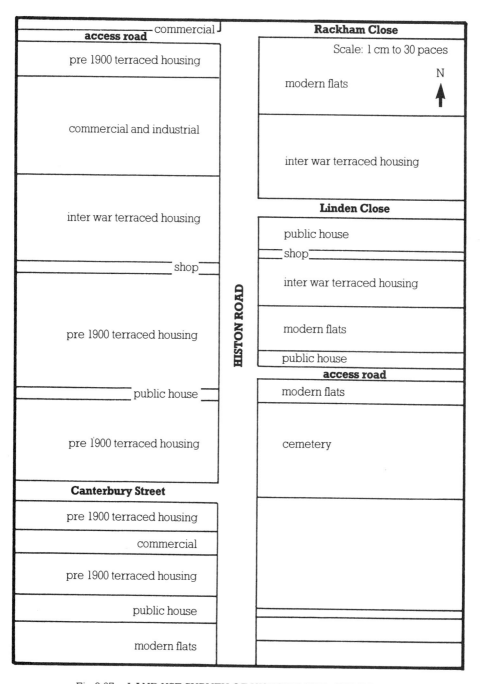

Fig 3.37 LAND USE SURVEY OF HISTON ROAD, CAMBRIDGE

1 Copy the section of Fig 3.37 which has been left blank and use the photograph to complete the labelling.

PART OF HISTON ROAD, CAMBRIDGE

IN THE CENTRE: 1

The city centre provides a wide range of opportunities for fieldwork study. This area is known as the Central Business District (C.B.D.) because it contains the large shops, offices, local government buildings and places of entertainment. Studies may range from trying to find the exact area of this district, to comparing its functions with other areas of the city, and discovering variations within the district.

Most studies will involve surveying the types of businesses, particularly the shops, found in the C.B.D. It is possible to simply write down what each shop in the district sells, but this presents problems. Some shops sell a wide variety of goods; some are large, others are small. What is needed is some way of grouping or classifying the wide variety of shops into manageable categories. One such classification is given here (see Fig 3.38). This classification not only deals with shops, but covers a range of functions which may be located in the C.B.D.

The letters to the left of the classification can be used as a key to carry out the survey. These may be marked on a map of the centre – an Ordnance Survey map at 1:1250 scale would be suitable (see page 78). Other information about the shop could be recorded simply by adding a letter or symbol: for instance, whether each were an independent shop or part of a chain of stores.

However, any survey of the C.B.D. will soon reveal that tall buildings have different functions on different floors. In the type of survey described above only the ground floor function has been considered. If the study being attempted requires a survey of the upper floor functions, then a different survey method is needed. For this the investigator should draw two vertical lines (to represent the street) down the centre of a page in a field notebook. Starting at the bottom of the page, each building can be marked with the ground floor function alongside the street and those on other floors to the side of it, as shown in Fig 3.39.

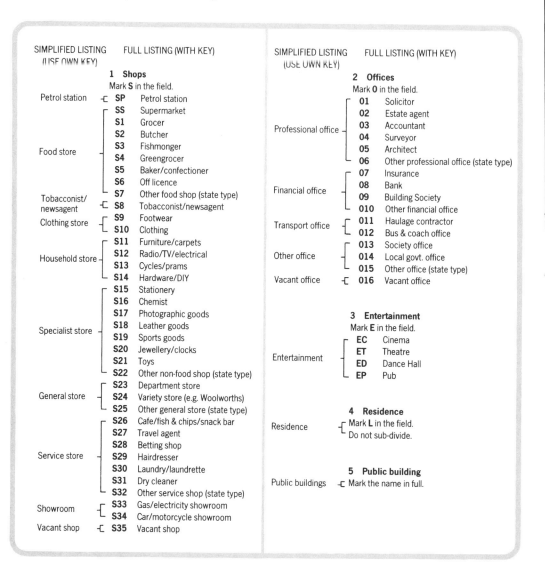

SIMPLIFIED LISTING (USE OWN KEY) / FULL LISTING (WITH KEY)

1 Shops
Mark **S** in the field.

Simplified	Code	Full listing
Petrol station	**SP**	Petrol station
Food store	**SS**	Supermarket
	S1	Grocer
	S2	Butcher
	S3	Fishmonger
	S4	Greengrocer
	S5	Baker/confectioner
	S6	Off licence
	S7	Other food shop (state type)
Tobacconist/newsagent	**S8**	Tobacconist/newsagent
Clothing store	**S9**	Footwear
	S10	Clothing
Household store	**S11**	Furniture/carpets
	S12	Radio/TV/electrical
	S13	Cycles/prams
	S14	Hardware/DIY
Specialist store	**S15**	Stationery
	S16	Chemist
	S17	Photographic goods
	S18	Leather goods
	S19	Sports goods
	S20	Jewellery/clocks
	S21	Toys
	S22	Other non-food shop (state type)
General store	**S23**	Department store
	S24	Variety store (e.g. Woolworths)
	S25	Other general store (state type)
Service store	**S26**	Cafe/fish & chips/snack bar
	S27	Travel agent
	S28	Betting shop
	S29	Hairdresser
	S30	Laundry/launderette
	S31	Dry cleaner
	S32	Other service shop (state type)
Showroom	**S33**	Gas/electricity showroom
	S34	Car/motorcycle showroom
Vacant shop	**S35**	Vacant shop

2 Offices
Mark **O** in the field.

Simplified	Code	Full listing
Professional office	**01**	Solicitor
	02	Estate agent
	03	Accountant
	04	Surveyor
	05	Architect
	06	Other professional office (state type)
Financial office	**07**	Insurance
	08	Bank
	09	Building Society
	010	Other financial office
Transport office	**011**	Haulage contractor
	012	Bus & coach office
Other office	**013**	Society office
	014	Local govt. office
	015	Other office (state type)
Vacant office	**016**	Vacant office

3 Entertainment
Mark **E** in the field.

Simplified	Code	Full listing
Entertainment	**EC**	Cinema
	ET	Theatre
	ED	Dance Hall
	EP	Pub

4 Residence

Residence — Mark **L** in the field. Do not sub-divide.

5 Public building

Public buildings — Mark the name in full.

Fig 3.38   CLASSIFICATION OF TOWN CENTRE FUNCTIONS

1 Give two ideas which could be tested in the C.B.D. by surveying the types of shops found there.

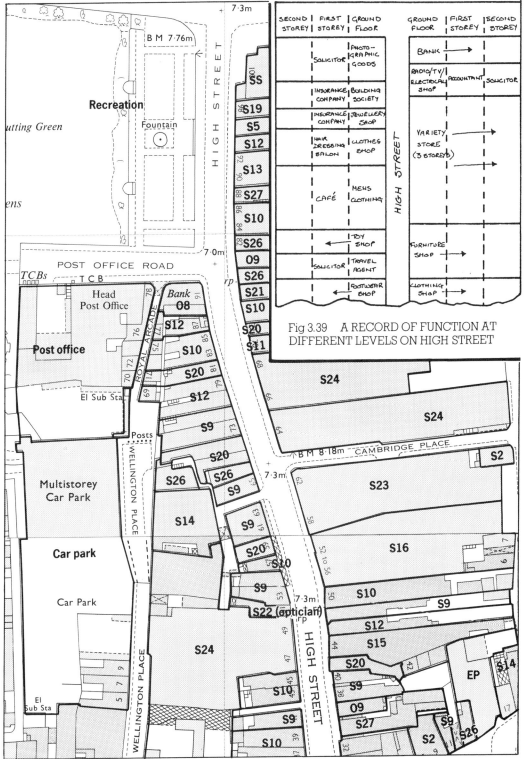

Fig 3.39 A RECORD OF FUNCTION AT DIFFERENT LEVELS ON HIGH STREET

SECOND STOREY	FIRST STOREY	GROUND FLOOR		GROUND FLOOR	FIRST STOREY	SECOND STOREY
	SOLICITOR	PHOTO-GRAPHIC GOODS		BANK →		
	INSURANCE COMPANY	BUILDING SOCIETY		RADIO/TV/ELECTRICAL SHOP	ACCOUNTANT	SOLICITOR
	INSURANCE COMPANY	JEWELLERY SHOP				
	HAIR DRESSING SALON	CLOTHES SHOP		VARIETY STORE (3 STOREYS) →		→
	CAFÉ	MENS CLOTHING				
	← TOY SHOP					
	SOLICITOR	TRAVEL AGENT		FURNITURE SHOP →		
	FOOTWEAR SHOP ←			CLOTHING SHOP →		

© Crown copyright 1983.
Reproduction in whole or in part by any means is prohibited without the prior permission of the Ordnance Survey.

Made and compiled by Ordnance Survey Southampton.

SURVEY OF PART OF THE CENTRAL BUSINESS DISTRICT OF WESTON-SUPER-MARE
(RECORDED ON 1:1250 ORDNANCE SURVEY MAPS ST 3161 NE AND ST 3261 NW)

IN THE CENTRE: 2

Geographers have suggested that the most desirable position for a shop in a town or city is in the centre of the C.B.D. at a road intersection. Because this is such a sought after location, the value of the land there is the highest in the town. This location is known as the Peak Land Value Intersection (P.L.V.I.). Many studies can stem from this idea. They include the following: that different types of shops are found at different distances from the P.L.V.I.; that height of buildings declines with distance from the P.L.V.I.; and that the number of pedestrians declines with distance from the P.L.V.I.

A measure of the land value of a property is the rates which it pays. The P.L.V.I. may therefore be found by discovering the location which pays the highest rates. This requires a study of the rateable values at the local Council Rating Office. This can be an awkward piece of work, so it may be advisable to ask a teacher or someone to give advice on how to obtain the information.

To look at the link between function and distance from the P.L.V.I. it would be best to take just five to ten functions or types of shop (for survey method see pages 76–7). Their distance from the P.L.V.I. could then be plotted and comparisons made.

The height of buildings may be surveyed using a similar method to that used to discover how function changes with height (see Fig 3.39). The number of storeys each building has can be plotted using this transect method.

Pedestrian counts may be used to test information about how people move and where they congregate within the C.B.D. The most straightforward method is to position people around the area which is being surveyed. Recorders should count those people passing a pre-arranged point and all should start and finish at the same time. A fifteen minute count will be enough to give results, the numbers being ticked off on a recording sheet. The information collected in this way may be mapped and isolines drawn (see page 125). A major problem with such a survey is that, to be done effectively, a large number of people is required to give adequate coverage of a town's central area. The time of day and indeed the day on which the survey is carried out are also of importance, as numbers of pedestrians vary quite considerably during the day and the week.

One other difficulty with a static count is that it only shows numbers at one point. This may be adequate for the study, but it is possible to discover how crowded areas of pavement or town are (i.e. the density of pedestrians) by carrying out a moving pedestrian survey. This is accomplished by walking at a steady even pace along 50–100 metre lengths of pavement. Pedestrians who pass, or are passed by the recorder should be counted, including those who have stopped to look in shop windows but who are not inside the shop. Each section of pavement should contain buildings with similar functions and no unusual gaps. The results may add to the information gained from a static count and can be recorded as a flow map (see pages 127–8). Alternatively, they could be used for detailed analysis of small areas of the C.B.D.

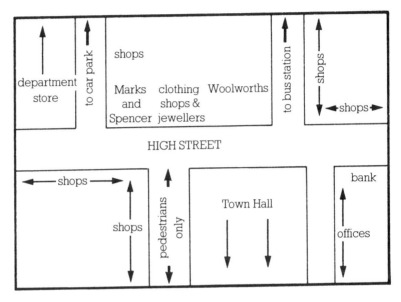

Fig 3.40   A TOWN CENTRE MAP

1   Several decisions need to be taken concerning pedestrian counts. Join with a neighbour and decide on the following, giving reasons in each case:
(a) Where would you position recorders for a static count in the area shown on Fig 3.40? (Assume that there are 8 recorders available.)
(b) At what time of day would you carry out the pedestrian count?
(c) What times of day would you *not* carry out the pedestrian count?
(d) Would you count everyone? If not, who would you ignore?
(e) What would you do if someone noticed what you were doing and began walking past the recorder several times?

IN THE CENTRE: 3

Shops selling one type of goods (for example, clothes shops) require different locations and have different selling techniques from other shops (for example, bookshops). These differences may cause the shops to have different frontages and may well cause shops of one type to group together in certain areas of the C.B.D.

A clothes shop selling fashion clothes for young people may well need a location in the area of highest pedestrian density. Such a shop may have no window display area, being open along its whole frontage to the street, to attract people in to buy and to create maximum sales area. Similarly, a jewellers will attract customers with its window display, also needing to be where large numbers of people will pass. The jewellers shop will often have a large window area in comparison to its frontage onto the street. This is achieved by making the display area funnel back into the shop, making it as long as possible at the expense of the sales area. Shoe shops and clothes shops are often on corners to achieve maximum display area.

The frontage is the length of the shop front along the street, and can be measured by pacing. It can be used as an indication of the size of the shop, with the larger shops having the larger frontages. An indication of the importance shops give to display area can be gained by comparing frontage with the length (paced) of the window display area of the shop. By dividing frontage by display area a display indicator can be arrived at. A figure of one or over will indicate maximum use of possible display area.

When devising ideas to test, one may suggest, for instance, that antique shops group together in one part of the C.B.D. But a more valuable study would involve discovering a reason or partial reason for what one finds out. It seems possible that antique shops would group in the older, historic part of the C.B.D. This could be tested by comparing a map of antique shops with one of the historic streets of the central area.

Some of the ideas mentioned earlier could be tested in a similar way. Do the clothes shops locate in areas of highest pedestrian density? Or is it that some clothes shops, for instance those selling young people's fashions, locate there and others locate elsewhere? Services such as Estate Agents also often locate close together in particular parts of the central area, as do Building Societies: which area do they choose? Why?

It is therefore worth looking round the C.B.D. before beginning a study, noticing patterns of where shops locate and then trying to think of one or two reasons for the pattern. Then an idea can be formed, which will not only be used to test whether the pattern is indeed present, but help to give reasons for the pattern.

Certain types of shops have more customers than others and will therefore need to be near the area of highest pedestrian density. Others, often specialist shops, may be located further from the area of highest pedestrian density; they require fewer customers and, because they are specialist shops, people are willing to travel further to them. Counting customers is one requirement of a study investigating these ideas. This can be achieved by standing opposite a row of shops (more than one shop could be investigated at once) and recording the number of customers entering the shop over a given time.

RETAILING

Towns and cities do not contain one shopping centre but several. These range from a small corner shop, to suburban centres consisting of a row of shops, to larger centres, and finally to the Central Business District itself. Then there are the large superstores or hypermarkets on the outskirts of the urban area, with large car parks catering for those who shop in bulk and use the car as a means of transport.

A comparison of two or more shopping centres can be made, studying the various features of the centres and the habits of the people who use them. The types of shops found in each shopping centre may be recorded on a map (see page 78). The size of the shops, represented by the length of the frontage and other features, may be recorded in the field notebook (see pages 78 and 82). The facilities provided at the centre may also be recorded: car parking, wide pavements, seats, bus stops and cycle routes all make shopping centres more attractive to customers.

A major feature of different shopping centres, however, is the type of people who use them. Where do the people come from? How do they travel to the area? How often do they come? What do they buy? Why do they use that centre, rather than another? These are all questions which only the people themselves can answer. Such a study will require the use of a questionnaire (see page 22) and should be undertaken at the least amount of inconvenience to the people involved.

One idea which is suggested by the first paragraph of this page is whether there is a hierarchy of centres within a town or city. This means whether there is an order of shopping centres from the largest (the Central Business District) to the smallest (the corner shop), and whether all the centres fit into a neat ordered pattern. A possible recording sheet for testing this idea is shown opposite; it records the number of businesses of different types in each centre in a town. In this way the number of establishments (shops, services, public houses etc.) and the number of functions position the centre within the hierarchy.

One problem with this approach is that it takes no account of the out of town hypermarket or superstore, which may have a wide variety of functions within one establishment. In this case the investigator may need to consider other factors: for instance, the number of people shopping at a centre, or the trade area of the centre (the area covered by the locations of the homes of those who use the centre).

Function	Location																
public houses & off licences																	
cafes																	
food shops: general																	
supermarket																	
fruit & veg.																	
freezer centre																	
bakery																	
fishmonger																	
fish & chips																	
butchers																	
delicatessen																	
sweets & tobacco																	
newsagents/stationery/fancy goods																	
pharmacy																	
clothing: men's																	
women's																	
children's																	
babywear & wool																	
general																	
footwear																	
services: filling station																	
hairdressers																	
cleaners																	
shoe repair																	
bank																	
insurance																	
betting shop																	
furniture																	
electrical/radio/TV																	
sports goods																	
luggage/leather goods																	
books & records																	
other retail (specify)																	
other services (specify)																	
total no. of establishments																	
total no. of functions																	

Fig 3.41   SUBURBAN SHOPPING CENTRES RECORDING SHEET

THE TOWN AND BEYOND

Towns and cities have a large influence on the lives of the people living in the surrounding villages. The people from the villages travel into the town for work, entertainment, shopping, and for the many services the town offers. The area over which the influence of the town extends is known as the 'urban field'.

There are a number of sources of information on the urban field of a town. One source is the people who live around the town. The investigator could stand in the central area of the town, which is the area visited by most people from the surrounding area, and research by means of questionnaires. Depending on the data required, the recorder could ask in which village the person lives, how they travel to the centre, how often they come, the reason for the visit and why they choose that particular town. It may also be possible to visit surrounding villages, asking people which town they visit.

Local bus services also indicate how far people come and how many people travel to a town. A timetable will provide a list of villages which are served by buses to the town. The number of buses each day will give some indication of the demand from a particular village (see Fig 3.42).

However, it is possible to find how far people travel, to shops for example, in another way. Many large stores deliver purchases to people's houses, and the delivery area provides a good indication of how far people travel to visit a particular shop.

A local newspaper, usually an evening, weekly or one of the free newspapers, is designed to serve the local area round a town. The number of times a place is mentioned in the course of a month can be counted. A daily evening paper may contain national news stories – these should be ignored for the purposes of the study. When the information is plotted on a local map, the area covered by the news stories is found, giving a good indication of the town's urban field. One problem which has to be decided upon is whether to include advertisements by businesses, or local advertising by readers, or just news stories. One or all of these could be used. Advertisements could be divided into groups: for example, shops, auto sales, general services, housing, and others.

A telephone directory will provide further information about homes and businesses. Major services (e.g. gas, water, electricity) which operate from large towns or cities will have maps of the area they serve. With the growth of local radio each station publishes a map of the area to which it is broadcasting. This is usually centred on the large town or city and is yet another example of a service provided for the surrounding area.

All these examples show how a picture of the area served or influenced by a large town or city may be built up. However, a word of caution is needed: many of these are areas designated by the service involved, partly for its own convenience. It would be interesting to see how far they matched the pattern revealed by the questionnaires, and how far the urban field was affected by fast transport routes like main roads or motorways.

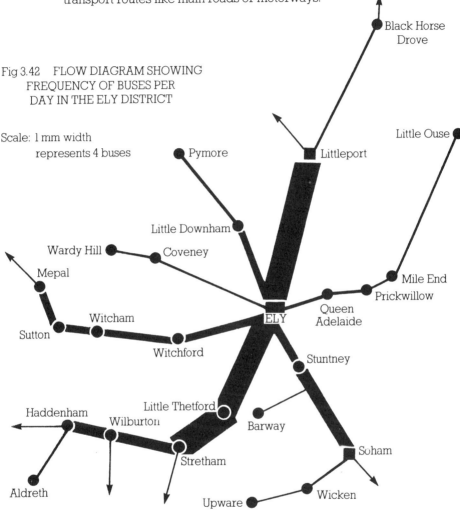

Fig 3.42   FLOW DIAGRAM SHOWING
FREQUENCY OF BUSES PER
DAY IN THE ELY DISTRICT

Scale: 1 mm width
represents 4 buses

1   (a) Design a questionnaire for use in the town centre to discover the extent of the urban field of a town and details of people's shopping habits. (See page 19 for information on designing questionnaires.)
(b) How would a questionnaire, used in the surrounding villages and requiring similar information, differ from that used in the town centre?

RURAL LAND USE

Transect from LOW FEN BRIDGE **to** HINTON WAY
Grid reference 479730 **to grid reference** 102757
Name of recorder ANNA Remus **Date** 23/8/83

Point	Location (grid ref.)	Land use	Geology	Soil	Height above sea level	Slope	Aspect	Distance from settlement/farm
45	482757	WHEAT	CLAY	CLAY	7 METRES	1°	SOUTH	500 M
44	481756	WHEAT	CLAY	CLAY	8 METRES	FLAT	–	400 M
43	481755	ORCHARD	SANDSTONE	SANDY	8 METRES	1°	SOUTH	300 M
42	481754	ORCHARD	SANDSTONE	SANDY	10 METRES	5°	SOUTH	200 M
41	481753	ORCHARD	SANDSTONE	SANDY	18 METRES	2°	SOUTH	100 M
40	482751	SETTLEMENT	SANDSTONE	SANDY	20 METRES	3°	SOUTH	0 m
39	483750	SETTLEMENT	SANDSTONE	SANDY	25 METRES	FLAT	–	0 m
38	484749	SETTLEMENT	SANDSTONE	SANDY	25 METRES	FLAT	–	0 m
37	484747	ORCHARD	SANDSTONE	SANDY	25 METRES	5°	SOUTH	100 m

Fig 3.43   PAGE FROM A NOTEBOOK FOR RECORDING LAND USE

The way in which the land outside towns is used is linked to many factors. It may be linked to both physical and human factors. Discovering which of them is the most important may well provide the basis of an investigation.

Before a link between land use and any factors can be established, information about the land use, altitude, slope, aspect, geology and climate needs to be collected. The problem here is how to cover a large enough area for the results to be worthwhile. Land use maps do exist (see page 25), as do maps of geology and soils. However, they do not cover the whole country, and may not contain all the information required. These maps would, however, be useful in the planning stages of an investigation.

As it is not possible to cover every part of an area in the investigation, some form of sampling is required. One method is to take a line sample (transect) across the area. By moving across an area, in as near a straight line as roads or footpaths allow, the land use may be marked on a base map. A map of 1:10 000 scale is best as it is not too cumbersome yet shows each of the fields. The amount of detail required in the categories of land use depends on the investigator. Two possibilities, one more detailed than the other, are shown in Fig 3.44. Other details can be included on the same map, so changes in rock type and soil could be noted; slope and aspect would be apparent from the map.

LIST A	LIST B
Settlement Industry Transport Derelict land	Settlement
Grassland	Grassland
Arable land	Arable land
Market gardening Orchards	Market gardening
Heath, moorland and rough land	Heath, moorland and rough land
Woodland	Woodland
Water and marsh Unvegetated Open space	Others

Fig 3.44   LAND USE CATEGORIES

A similar survey may be undertaken using a recording sheet rather than a map. Having chosen a line or transect across the area, the land use and other factors which the investigator wishes to record are noted at regular intervals. This is a form of line sampling (see page 18). The recording sheet (see Fig 3.43) is completed (starting at the bottom of the page) every 100 metres along the line of the transect, the metres being measured by pacing. Material gathered in this way may be analysed relatively easily.

Land use may also be investigated by recording details at points selected randomly over an area (although this should be modified if geology is to be considered, see pages 17–18). There are, however, drawbacks to this method, as one may find problems of access to some areas of land.

The recording sheet shown here includes columns for investigating any link between land use and physical factors such as geology, soils, height, aspect and slope. Methods of collecting information concerning these factors are found on pages 39–44. The final column is being used to investigate whether land use changes with distance from a farm or settlement. This may be estimated either on the ground or from the map, using groups of distances: for example, 0–250, 251–500, 501–750, 751–1000, over 1000 metres. It may be that, in areas with similar physical factors, the human factor of distance influences land use. Why may this be so? It should, however, be remembered that the use made of any piece of land may result from several factors. A detailed investigation into the use of a small area of land, involving discussion with those who use the land, may be possible.

In rural areas remember the Country Code and do not go onto private land without permission.

ON THE FARM

Think about a field that you know well, perhaps one you pass on the way to school each day or one you use for picnics. What is the field used for? Why is it used in that way? What work does the farmer do in the field each year? How does this field compare with the other fields on the farm? Such questions may be answered from fieldwork concerned with a study of farming.

The first stage of such a study, as with all fieldwork, is to design a statement to test or a question to answer. In the case of a farm study this is not easy. It is important to avoid the trap of simply finding out all you can about the farm with no aim in mind. Possible statements to test in the case of a dairy farm might be:

– that the farm fits the input/output diagram of a dairy farm (see Fig 3.45). This will involve finding out about the inputs and outputs by observation and questionnaires, and adding or deleting parts of the diagram.

– that the farm is in a good location for a dairy farm. This will involve finding what the most important factors are for the location of a dairy farm and testing these for the chosen farm.

– that the land use on the farm varies with distance from the farm buildings. This will require making a land use map and thinking of a

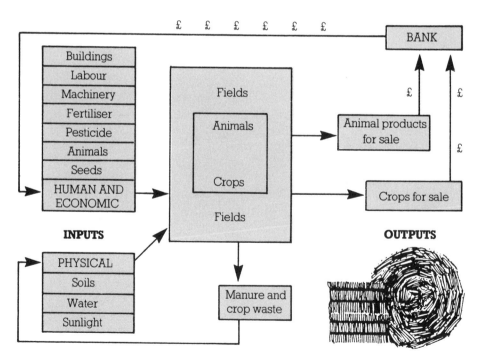

Fig 3.45   INPUT/OUTPUT DIAGRAM OF A DAIRY FARM

---

method of comparing land use with distance from the buildings. It also poses the question that if it is correct, why is it correct? Perhaps the farmer will need to be consulted. Does he keep cows near the milking parlour where he needs to take them twice a day, and use the fields further away for fodder crops? If the statement is incorrect, then what does determine what grows where?

– that the land use on the farm is mainly influenced by the climate of the area.

There are three methods involved in collecting the information for these studies. Firstly, the land use may be plotted on a map of the farm, as was done for the top map on page 26.

Secondly, fieldwork measurement may be required to test height, slope, aspect, soils, geology and climate (see pages 29–44). A plan of the farm buildings and a record of the type of machinery used may well help with finding out about the methods used on the farm.

Land use and extent of the farm
Farm buildings (and their use)
Labour (workers)
Machinery (and its use)
Fertiliser ⎫
Pesticide ⎬ (type, source of supply)
Seeds ⎭
Animals (type and number)
Soil (types and where found)
Water (any irrigation or
  drainage)
Crops (where each sold)
Animal products (where sold)
The work on the farm (i.e. the
  work towards each product and
  methods employed)

Finally, the farmer may be consulted. A questionnaire should be written out before the visit. As with all questionnaires, it should be brief and concerned only with the aspects being studied. This may be done after a preliminary visit has shown which points need to be asked. A checklist of some of the points which may be raised is shown here (see Fig 3.46), but not all will be needed for any one study.

Remember to arrange a time with the farmer when it would be convenient to visit the farm, as he will certainly be busy. Always ask permission before visiting the farm.

Fig 3.46　ON THE FARM – CHECKLIST

1　Make a list of what you would need to study if you were testing the idea that the land use on the farm is mainly influenced by the climate of the area.
2　Write out the questionnaire you would use to help to test the idea that the farm fits the input/output diagram of a dairy farm. You will need to decide which aspects of the diagram you would test by observation and which you would test by questionnaire.

THE WORLD OF WORK

The world of work is an extremely important part of people's lives, and the type of work or industry located in a place can affect its whole character. Industry may be divided into the primary sector (concerned mainly with obtaining raw materials), the secondary sector (concerned with making something) and the tertiary sector (concerned with offering a service). A survey in school may be used to discover which sector is most important in the local area. By asking a sample of the members of the school in which sector of industry their parents or friends work, a pattern may be quickly established.

A more detailed study within a town, city or area will involve a survey of local industry. However, such is the variety of industries that some form of grouping or classification is essential. One method of classification is shown below (Fig 3.47). This list may be reduced either by concentrating on certain categories or by grouping some together. Trade directories are published for many towns and from these it may be possible to plot the type of industries on a map to discover patterns of location. One problem may be that the industries are entered by name and the type of industry is not apparent. The local library would contain such directories. A telephone directory would also give similar information.

Industry		**Commerce**	
I/X	Extractive (mines, quarries etc.)	S	Shops
T	Textiles	M	Markets
E	Engineering & metal trades	OF	Offices
F	Food, drink & tobacco	BA	Banks
D	Dress (clothing & footwear)	WA	Warehouses, coal yards etc.
C	Chemicals		
P	Paper, printing & publishing		
V	Vehicles		**Other Services**
L	Leather & fur		
BR	Bricks, pottery, glass, cement etc.	S/T	Transport
W	Wood, timber, furniture	G	Garages
B	Building construction	H/I	Hotels, inns, cafes etc.
TE	Technology (computers, radios, instruments)	OS	Other
O	Other (e.g. rubber, plastics etc.)		

Fig 3.47   CLASSIFICATION OF INDUSTRY AND COMMERCE

For a larger town or city this method would prove rather impractical. A field survey may prove more useful. To find the location of various types of industry a method like that described on page 73 could be used. In this case each square would need to contain the dominant type of industry. Many squares would contain residential areas only and could be left blank. The areas with a lot of industry could be subdivided to give more accuracy. For a larger city a transect (see page 87) would be more convenient.

By undertaking a field survey more information could be recorded. Industry could be divided into heavy industry (that which involves the use of large factories, processing raw materials, e.g. iron and steel or chemicals, or making large items) and light industry (small factories and workshops making relatively small items). The size of the factory could be surveyed by pacing its frontage along the road or by working out its area from a map. Such data could provide information about the pattern of industry in a town. It is then possible to make a more detailed study of individual areas or factories (see The Place of Work).

The type of industry or work undertaken in a place may change. In a town or city this could be investigated in a small area. In rural areas a village provides a suitable unit for investigation. Kelly's Directory could be used to provide information about the work and industry patterns in a village fifty years ago and this could be compared with fieldwork observation of patterns today.

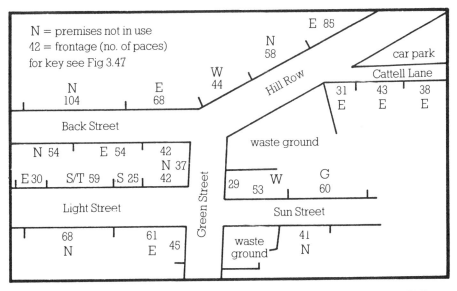

Fig 3.48 INDUSTRIAL SURVEY OF PART OF A CITY IN NORTHERN ENGLAND

THE PLACE OF WORK

There is a tremendous variety of places where people work. These range from the home or small office working with one or two other people to large factories. Try to make a list of twenty very different places where people work.

This section deals with the possibility of studying some kind of manufacturing industry, but could be adapted to investigate other types of workplace. Studying this topic may well involve a visit to the works or factory and a guided tour by someone who works there. If this is the case, the investigator should write a letter to the company requesting a visit. The letter should outline the reason for the request and give a wide choice of time when the visit could take place.

If the request is granted, then the investigator will need to make very careful preparations. A specific list of questions should be drawn up, the choice depending on the investigation being undertaken. A checklist of possible topics is given here (Fig 3.49). The investigator should arrive at the factory at the correct time, be polite and be well equipped with questions, pencils and clipboard. Interest should be shown at each stage in the visit, even in sections which are not relevant to the study. Take the opportunity to find out everything; there may be things relevant to the study which you had not thought of before. The question checklist will help, and it is a good idea to answer them during the tour, completing the unanswered questions at the end. If the guide sees that the fieldworker is well prepared and interested, then he is much more likely to be helpful.

REMEMBER: only ask for a tour of the factory if the information cannot be obtained in any other way.

The question of location of the factory and how far it conforms to the input-output diagram of an industry

Location of factory – date established
– original reason for location
– position today
– site

Size of works – area of site
– number of employees
– size, shape, function of buildings

Inputs – raw materials – origin
– previous processing
– method of transport
– water supply
– power supply
– number of female/male employees

Process – how the raw materials are made into finished products

Outputs – finished products
– markets for finished products
– waste – waste disposal
– method of transport

Special points to note – e.g. problems of site, noise, pollution etc.

Fig 3.49   CHECKLIST OF TOPICS FOR INVESTIGATING INDUSTRY

(Fig 3.50) may be investigated in this way. An idea to test should be carefully thought out to avoid the possibility of simply writing a story of the firm.

There are some aspects of the industry which firms may be reluctant to provide. For instance, a study of the pattern of the employees' journeys to work may not be possible, as it would be unusual for a firm to give an investigator access to home addresses. This type of investigation is best avoided.

Often the processes involved in factories are very complicated. The range of different operations undertaken to make an item may be difficult to record. One way of overcoming this difficulty is to use a flow diagram technique for recording (Fig 3.51).

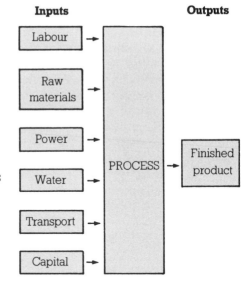

Fig 3.50   INPUT/OUTPUT DIAGRAM OF INDUSTRY

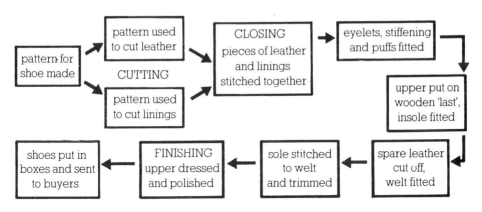

Fig 3.51   FLOW DIAGRAM OF SHOE MANUFACTURING

1   (a) With the help of a friend produce an idea to test which involves mining or quarrying.
(b) Imagine that the investigation into your idea involved a visit to the mine or quarry. Write a letter asking the manager if you could have permission for the visit.
(c) Make a list of the questions you would ask during the visit.

TRANSPORT
TRAFFIC IN TOWN

The movement of traffic within a town is something which concerns everyone. New traffic systems are constantly being devised to try to avoid congestion and to plan for the continually increasing car ownership, the size of goods vehicles and the needs of cyclists and pedestrians.

Traffic flow along a route may be recorded by taking a traffic census, that is counting vehicles passing along the route during a certain period of time. The flow may vary at different points along the route and consequently it is important to choose the census point with care. Traffic will also vary with the time of day and this may provide a focus for the investigation. Preliminary surveys will indicate the best times of day to carry out the census and counts between 15 and 30 minutes should prove adequate.

The investigation may be concerned with how well the road can take the volume of traffic moving along it and whether there is congestion. In this case it will only be necessary to take a census at the peak time of flow. This will be from 8a.m. to 9.30a.m. and 5p.m. to 6.30p.m. on weekdays as people go to or from work.

A lorry will take up more road space than a car or bicycle and will cause more wear and tear on the road. This can be used to provide a measure of overcrowding by recording the volume of traffic along a route according to size. If each car is one Passenger Car Unit (P.C.U.), then a bus or lorry may be counted as 3 P.C.U.s and a bicycle or

Name of recorder ANNA BROWN	Town CAMBRIDGE
Position MILTON RD. / ARBURY RD. JUNCTION	Direction of traffic SOUTH
Date 24 FEBRUARY 1984	Time from 8.00 AM to 8.30 AM

Bicycles	Motor-cycles, scooters	Cars	Light commercial vehicles – vans, minibuses etc.	Heavy commercial vehicles – lorries, tractors, buses, etc.
卌 卌 卌 III	卌 卌 卌 卌	卌 卌 卌 卌 卌 卌 / 卌 卌 卌 卌 卌 卌 / 卌 卌 卌 卌 卌 卌 / 卌 卌 卌 卌 卌 卌 / 卌 卌 I	卌 卌 卌	卌 卌 卌 卌 卌

Fig 3.52   RECORDING SHEET SHOWING NUMBER OF VEHICLES TRAVELLING ALONG A ROAD IN A HALF HOUR SURVEY PERIOD

motorcycle as ½ P.C.U. The results of the survey may be compared with official maximums for different types of road. These are as follows:

375 P.C.U.s per hour for a 7.3 m 2 lane carriageway
688 P.C.U.s per hour for a 10.0 m 3 lane carriageway
1512 P.C.U.s per hour for a 14.6 m dual 2 lane carriageway

In order to carry out investigations into traffic flows along roads, it is useful to divide the vehicles into some form of grouping or classification. This is usually done according to type and size of vehicle. One possible grouping is used in the traffic census sheet shown here (Fig. 3.52). Others could be devised which concentrate on private or commercial vehicles.

A traffic census of whatever kind does involve the investigator being near a roadside. Great care should be taken. The investigator should choose a point with a good view of the road, but well back from the road where there is no danger, and where a driver's view is not distracted (as it would be, for instance, on corners).

1   What type of vehicle might have a P.C.U. value of 2?
2   The recording sheet (Fig 3.52) shows the number of vehicles per hour travelling along a 7.3 m 2 lane carriageway. Work out whether this road would be congested according to the official figures. Note that the recorder only recorded traffic flowing in one direction.

TRANSPORT
OUT OF TOWN

Transport movement not only occurs within towns but between places as well. Bus and rail timetables can provide a great deal of information.

Bus timetables can be used to find how strong the links are between one place and another. Most bus stations have maps showing the routes the buses take. These routes can be plotted on a base map and flow lines drawn according to the number of buses travelling along each (see page 86). This will give an indication of how heavily used the individual routes are. Linking this information with the population of places may provide the basis for a study.

There are fluctuations in the number of buses running on different routes at various times in the day. These may be obtained by counting the number of buses running each hour between places as shown on the timetable. The information when graphed (see page 110) can be compared with traffic flows.

Finding how long the journey would take leads to investigation of how well places are linked in terms of time (e.g. how long it takes to get from surrounding villages to a main centre). Using the bus timetables, the time taken to get from each village to the main town or city can be plotted on a map next to the village. By drawing isolines (see page 126) a pattern can be displayed. Questions such as, 'Does it take longer to reach the centre from some places than from others, despite it being a similar or shorter distance?' can be answered.

Railway passenger timetables will give similar information and can produce interesting results. For instance, the time taken for the rail journey from Newcastle to Liverpool (a distance of 200 km) is four hours, and the time taken to travel from Newcastle to London (a distance of 400 km) is three and a quarter hours.

One major problem in working with traffic flows is that it is difficult to discover where a vehicle has come from, and whether its destination is the town or whether it is just passing through. The names and addresses of the home town or city often found on the side of lorries may help to give some indication of where they have come from. This of course will give little indication of destination unless the survey is carried out at a major destination for lorries such as a port. It also means that the information gathered from a large number of lorries needs to be plotted on the map before a pattern can be established with any degree of certainty.

Car registration numbers can also give an indication of where the vehicle was first licensed. Unfortunately the A.A. handbook no longer contains this information, but it can be found in a small booklet, 'Vehicle Index Marks in the British Isles', which is published by the A.A.

By plotting the information on a map, a pattern of points of origin could be established, as could the proportions of local and visiting traffic. However, a large number of vehicles would need to be plotted to gain any degree of certainty: for as cars change owners, so they move from one part of the country to another.

Mepal, Green	0708	0735	0814	0925	....	1125	1230	1325	1455	1625	1815
Sutton, Ship	0713	0740	0820	0930	0935	1130	1235	1330	1500	1630	1820
Witcham, Village	0720	....	0827	0937	....	1137	1241	1337	1507	....	....
Witcham, Toll	0722	0744	0829	0939	0940	1139	1243	1339	1509	1635	1825
Witchford St. Andrew's Hall	0728	....	0835	....	0946	1145	....	1345	1515	1641	1831
ELY, Market Street	0738	....	0845	....	0956	1155	....	1355	1525	1651	1839

Fig 3.53   PART OF A BUS TIMETABLE

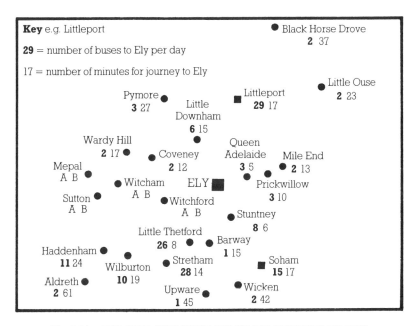

Fig 3.54   NUMBER AND JOURNEY TIMES OF BUSES TO ELY
FROM SURROUNDING VILLAGES

1   Use the section of a bus timetable given here to:
(a) Find the number of buses on this route in one day which would be inserted at the points marked A on the map.
(b) Find the time taken by buses to reach the city centre from each of the villages on this route, which would be inserted at the points marked B on the map.
Discuss your findings with a friend.

HOW DO WE SEE PLACES?

NEIGHBOURHOOD FACILITIES

Ask yourself how many metres or kilometres it is to school or to a place which you know well, then ask yourself how long it takes you to get there by whatever form of transport you take. Which do you think is the more accurate method of measuring distance?

Supposing you tried to find out which area people thought of as their neighbourhood – would all the people from one area give the same answer? Would they be able to mark its boundaries? Or, supposing you tried to find out which parts of their town or city people knew best, would they all give the same answer, or would your results show differences according to age, sex or where they lived or worked?

Do all people think that the same areas of the town or countryside are equally attractive? What makes one area more attractive than others? For instance, which shopping centre do you use? Why do you use that one and not others? Is it simply because it is the most convenient or are there other reasons?

Questions like these help us to understand people's views about the place in which they live. Many geographers feel that what a place is like to live in is equally important as the way in which it is arranged. An investigation of these questions will mean asking people to answer questions or mark places on a map, and how this is to be done needs to be considered carefully (see page 19).

Finding out the extent of the area people see as their neighbourhood requires the use of a large scale map. This map should have the streets clearly named and some other details, but too much information will make it difficult to read. The investigator could begin the study by mapping areas of similar housing types, for example of similar age, size, design and tenure. Then the investigator could take a large scale map to an area of similar housing type and ask people to draw a line round what they consider to be their neighbourhood. A comparison of the two maps could show whether house type is important in determining people's idea of neighbourhood. It may also show how important open space, main roads, or other breaks in the housing are in providing boundaries of a neighbourhood.

One problem with asking people to draw lines on maps is not only that one needs a lot of maps but also that people may well have difficulty in being so precise. When people think of a neighbourhood they tend to think of fixed points, for instance, a friend's home, a shop or a church, as being inside or outside an area. So another method of finding out the information is to mark a series of prominent features on the map and ask people which they consider to be inside or outside their neighbourhood. A line drawn around those which the majority feel are inside the neighbourhood would mark the boundaries.

A similar method could be used when finding out which parts of a town people visit most, or know best. In addition, people could be asked how often they walk past particular prominent features in a town. With all studies of this kind it is important that people are not prompted by the investigator. After all it is what the people think, not what the questioner thinks, that matters!

'Oh yes, all the houses in my neighbourhood have white fences'

1 Join with a friend to write down the steps you would take to investigate the idea that, 'People of different age groups from the same area make regular use of different parts of the town or city in which they live'.

THE QUALITY OF RURAL AND URBAN ENVIRONMENTS

The photographs **A** and **B** show two very different rural environments. Which area would you prefer to visit or to live in? Having made a judgement, try to discuss or think about why you preferred that area. Could you list a number of reasons for your choice?

You may have chosen photograph **A** because it was quiet and peaceful with attractive views. Remember though that you would be looking at the area as a visitor; someone who lives there might feel that it was isolated and boring. A miner might well choose photograph **B** because he could find a job there.

Geographers are increasingly concerned with the quality of the environment: whether it is an attractive or pleasant area to visit or to live and work in. This is important for everyone, but particularly so in the case of a National Park which is planning to maintain the attractiveness of an area whilst providing amenities for those who live there and for visitors. An interest in the quality of the environment makes people aware of the importance of living in pleasant surroundings.

What may be attractive to one person may not be attractive to another. In such cases we could find a majority viewpoint. Sometimes one group may find an area attractive whilst another may not; this could provide an interesting study in itself.

To discover how people feel about an area and the quality of the environment is not easy, as it is difficult to put into words – or indeed to reach general agreement. However, one way which has been used quite successfully is to:

(a) Make a list of about 12 to 15 pairs of words which describe opposite views of aspects of the quality of the environment. (See examples 1 and 2.)

(b) Each group is then scored on a scale from +3 to −3.

(c) The scores are added together.

(d) The higher the score the better the quality of the environment. Group scores can be added together and used in a similar way.

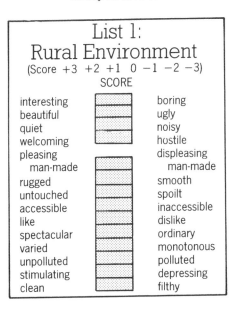

1   Try using the lists to test the quality of the environments shown in photographs **A** and **B**, and photographs **C** and **D**.

STREETSCAPES

PART OF
DE FREVILLE
AVENUE

Although an environment survey gives an overall impression of a town, it does not give any idea of how the areas of a town differ in detail. For small areas this may be achieved by streetscape mapping.

The technique is best used to map a small area rather than a single street. It may be used to compare districts of a town or to provide evidence about one particular district. It is necessary to mark on the map the main features which make up the environment, in order to build up a description of the area being studied. To do this, symbols are used which may be easily understood when the overall pattern is interpreted. A list of features and suggested symbols are shown here (Fig 3.55) with an example of a completed map (right).

Some of the features are already shown on Ordnance Survey maps of 1:1250 and 1:2500 scale and therefore are not listed here. For example, whether the houses are detached, semi-detached or terraced, the size of the garden and width of road would all be shown.

STREETSCAPE MAPPING OF
DE FREVILLE AVENUE, BASED ON
1:1250 ORDNANCE SURVEY MAP TL 4559

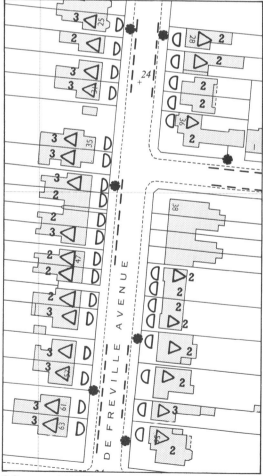

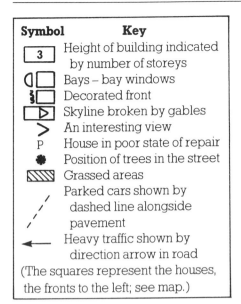

Symbol	Key
3	Height of building indicated by number of storeys
◖☐	Bays – bay windows
⫶☐	Decorated front
☐▷	Skyline broken by gables
>	An interesting view
P	House in poor state of repair
✸	Position of trees in the street
▨▨	Grassed areas
⁄ ⁄ ⁄	Parked cars shown by dashed line alongside pavement
←	Heavy traffic shown by direction arrow in road

(The squares represent the houses, the fronts to the left; see map.)

Fig 3.55   STREETSCAPE: LIST OF FEATURES

The information for the example shown was recorded directly onto a copy of the map. This may not always be practical and it may be easier to produce a field notebook page where each feature can be entered in columns, either for each house or each section of the street. Field sketching of typical houses will help to provide an overall picture of the area, as will details of type of building, surveys of building materials and age of houses (see page 66).

However, even after this has been done, the investigator may still need to decide whether the townscape is desirable or not. This will obviously depend on who is deciding, but the environment survey suggested on page 102 may give some indication.

A special feature of a town or city, such as a shopping centre, may be judged using a mixture of an environment survey and a streetscape survey. The environment survey technique (see page 102) may be used to look at design of the centre, ease of parking, ease of movement round the centre, visual appearance, range of goods sold, price, and atmosphere. Others could be added to the list. People could be asked to give scores from +2 to −2 for features under each of these headings; examples for design and atmosphere are given here (Fig 3.56).

Design	Well designed	+2	+1	0	−1	−2	Badly designed
	Simple layout	+2	+1	0	−1	−2	Complicated layout
	Designed with shopper in mind	+2	+1	0	−1	−2	Not designed with shopper in mind
	Wide covered walkways	+2	+1	0	−1	−2	Walkways open and narrow
Atmosphere	Busy	+2	+1	0	−1	−2	Not busy
	Personal	+2	+1	0	−1	−2	Impersonal
	Friendly atmosphere	+2	+1	0	−2	−2	Unfriendly atmosphere

Fig 3.56   SHOPPING CENTRE FEATURES

1 Make a copy of the part of the map of De Freville Avenue, Cambridge, which is not completed. Use the photograph to label the streetscape features of that part of the street.
2 Make your own chart for judging the shopping centre features of visual appearance, using Fig 3.56 as a guide.

PRESSURES ON THE COUNTRYSIDE

The countryside is used by a wide variety of people for a number of different activities, some of which are shown in the cartoon above. Often the quality of the environment in rural areas depends on how these people use or abuse the area.

Agriculture, industry and housing in the countryside can be investigated using techniques described elsewhere in this book. Such investigations can be directed towards how each is changing the area and its effects on the countryside, using an environment survey. It is tempting to think of investigating chemical pollution of the soil or rivers, or of dust or other pollution from industry. However, this should be discussed with science teachers who could advise on how worthwhile such an investigation might be.

Perhaps the greatest pressure on the countryside comes from the people who visit it for leisure. When people visit an area they tend to collect in certain well known beauty spots or at places which provide facilities and activities for them. To find out about these tourists, where they come from, how they travelled or how often they come, it is necessary to use a questionnaire (see page 20). However, investigating tourism at a particular spot or village can also involve surveys of facilities available, and an environment survey to try to find out what makes that place so attractive. The effects of the tourists can provide interesting studies, plotting the position of signs which would not be there if tourists did not come, and the car parking facilities or restrictions which are felt to be necessary.

In this country most of the visitors to rural areas may well travel by car. In addition to traffic counts (see pages 95–6), it should be possible to investigate the effects of a large influx of vehicles. There will be increased provision of car parking places in villages and at picnic sites. But there will also be roadside parking which may well wear away (erode) the vegetation on the verges. The area of a number of these patches could be found by measuring the length of each along the roadside and multiplying by the average of four widths (distances from the roadside to the edge of the patch). From the amount of wear over a specific distance, the type of road and the lengths of different types of road in the area, a picture of the effect of roadside parking could be worked out.

Wherever tourists collect there is pressure on the countryside. The number of tourists at a particular site could be measured at different times. The effects of numbers of people following particular paths (footpath erosion) can be measured in the same way as for roadside parking. But perhaps the most noticeable effect is that of litter. By counting the amount and type of litter, and comparing this with tourist numbers, some measure of its effect may be worked out.

There is also the possibility of investigating the likely effects of new proposals. The building of a new leisure attraction could be investigated, looking at the pressures from the extra visitors, their cars, the effect on the landscape, employment and housing in the area. Investigation of each of these could be based on the present situation and some viewpoint developed.

---

1 How would you develop an investigation into the impact of roadside parking in a tourist area?

2 What factors would you investigate if you were undertaking a study of the effects of building a new reservoir in a rural valley which is popular with tourists?

PART 3: COLLECT AND RECORD, ENVIRONMENTAL TOPICS

WHAT IS THE MOST USUAL NUMBER?
THE MEAN, MEDIAN AND MODE

An interesting study which can be carried out is to find out how long it takes vehicles to pass through a town. This will be affected by the amount of congestion in the town and it may vary through the day. The technique described could also be used to discover how much of the town's traffic was passing straight through on its way to somewhere else and how much was visiting the town.

The technique involves recording the time at which each vehicle travelling along a main road enters the town. This is possible by taking the registration number of each vehicle and noting the time it passes the 30 m.p.h. speed restriction signs at the edge of the town. Other recorders note the time and registration numbers of vehicles leaving the town. All recorders need to synchronise their watches, and minor roads can be ignored for the purposes of the survey. Those recording vehicles leaving the town will need to finish later than those recording vehicles entering.

The two sets of information may be compared and vehicles which enter, but do not leave the town, may be assumed to be visiting the town. The time taken for a vehicle to cross the town, the transit time, may be tabulated.

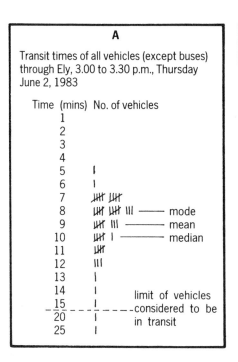

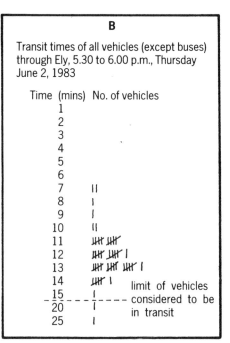

Fig 4.1   TRANSIT TIMES RECORDED IN ELY FOR TWO HALF HOUR INTERVALS

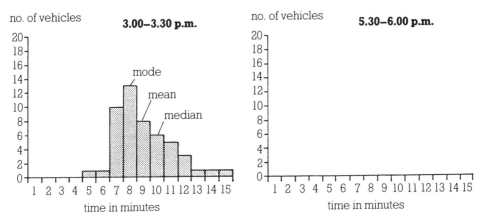

Fig 4.2   BAR CHART OF TRANSIT TIMES THROUGH ELY

A table for one such survey, for the City of Ely, is shown in Fig 4.1.
The question which now arises is what is the most usual time it takes
for a vehicle to pass through Ely between 3.00 and 3.30 p.m.?

One way of answering this question is to find the average, or **mean**,
time it takes. To find the mean, all the times are added together and
divided by the number of times recorded. In this case the total of all
the times is 450 mins and the number of times is 50, so the mean
equals 450 ÷ 50 = 9 mins.

However, a look at the table (Fig 4.1 A) will show that this is not the
middle time on the list. Indeed the middle time is 10 mins. This figure
is known as the **median**.

Finally, neither the mean nor the median figure are the same as the
time taken by the most vehicles. Thirteen vehicles took 8 mins in
transit; this figure is known as the **mode**.

Each of these – the mean, median and mode – is a valid method
of finding the 'most usual' number in a set of figures. It may be helpful
to compare each with similar figures for a different time of day
(as in Fig 4.1B).

---

1   Look at the figures for vehicles in transit from 5.30 to 6.00 p.m.
on Thursday June 2, 1983 in Ely (Fig 4.1 B). Work out the mean,
median and mode of these figures.
2   Draw a graph of the figures similar to that drawn for the traffic
from 3.00 to 3.30 p.m. on that day (Fig 4.2).
3   Compare the two sets of results – what do you notice?
4   Join with a friend (a) to discuss why the differences shown
may have occurred and (b) to work out an idea which could be
tested using this technique.

GRAPHS AND CHARTS
THE BAR CHART, HISTOGRAM AND PIE CHART

A recent fieldwork exercise in East Anglia investigated the idea that, 'Hospital facilities in rural counties like Norfolk are becoming increasingly inaccessible'. As part of the investigation the group used bus timetables to record the number of buses passing through the villages in the survey area on their way to King's Lynn, where the nearest hospital was located. The results of their survey are recorded in the table opposite (Fig 4.3).

One way of presenting these results is to draw a bar chart. This involves little processing of the data and is simply a way of presenting it in the form of a graph. As can be seen from Fig 4.4, each individual piece of information is plotted. Such a graph would have little value if large amounts of data were being presented.

The results of a survey may be seen more clearly if a histogram is used to present the data. A histogram is constructed in a similar way to a bar chart, but the data are grouped together. The data in the case of the buses to King's Lynn range from 1 to 176. The data on the number of buses may be grouped together in groups of ten; the groups would then be 0–10, 11–20, 21–30, 31–40, 41–50, over 50. Notice that no number appears in two groups. The number of times villages appear in each group would be:

No. of buses	No. of villages
0–10	3
11–20	3
21–30	1
31–40	1
41–50	2
over 50	2

From these figures a histogram is drawn, as shown in Fig 4.5. This has the advantage of making the information easier to read, but we do not know details of individual villages.

If the villages considered accessible were those with over 30 buses passing through each week, then this information may be read from either graph. How many of the villages could be considered accessible? Which graph provides the answer most easily?

Village	Number of buses to King's Lynn each week
1	89
2	49
3	49
4	34
5	20
6	176
7	3
8	18
9	17
10	2
11	29
12	1

Fig 4.3   NUMBER OF BUSES TRAVELLING TO KING'S LYNN EACH WEEK FROM NEARBY VILLAGES

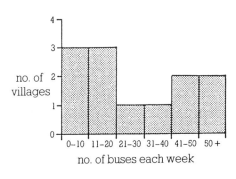

Fig 4.5   HISTOGRAM OF THE NUMBER OF BUSES TRAVELLING TO KING'S LYNN EACH WEEK FROM NEARBY VILLAGES

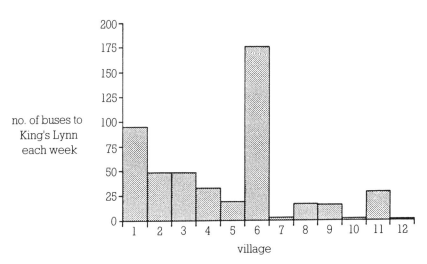

Fig 4.4   BAR CHART OF THE NUMBER OF BUSES TRAVELLING TO KING'S LYNN EACH WEEK FROM NEARBY VILLAGES

PART 4: PROCESSING AND PRESENTING THE DATA

In the course of the same survey the team asked people whether they were satisfied with the hospitals serving the district. The results are shown in Fig 4.7. This kind of information, as well as that dealing with numbers in groups, may be presented as a pie chart. A circle is drawn which is divided into sectors depending on the size of each group. In the example the number of those satisfied with the hospital services is 177; that is, 177 out of 506. There are 360° in a circle. With this information the following formula will help you to work out the size of the sector:

size of sector = $\dfrac{\text{number of degrees in a circle}}{\text{total number of factors}} \times$ number to be in this sector

In this case it is: $\dfrac{360}{506} \times 177 = 126°$

The formula is even easier if you have the figures in percentages: each 1% is 3.6° on the chart, so 35% would be 3.6 × 35 = 126°. The completed pie chart is shown below (Fig 4.6) and it indicates clearly that most people (76%) were satisfied with the service.

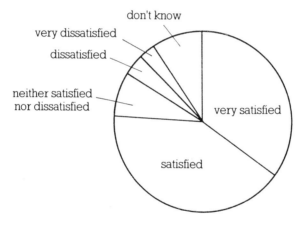

Fig 4.6   PIE CHART OF SATISFACTION WITH HOSPITALS
SERVING THE DISTRICT

	Number	**Percentage**	**Sector size**
Very satisfied	177	35	126°
Satisfied	207	41	148°
Neither satisfied			
nor dissatisfied	41	8	29°
Dissatisfied	23	4	14°
Very dissatisfied	14	3	11°
Don't know	44	9	32°

Fig 4.7   SATISFACTION WITH HOSPITALS SERVING THE DISTRICT

AROUND THE CENTRE

STAR DIAGRAMS AND RADIAL CHARTS

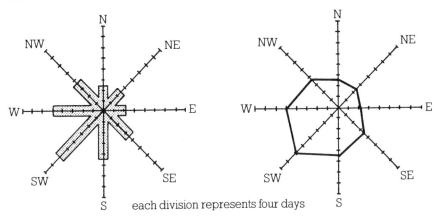

Fig 4.8   A WIND ROSE

Fig 4.9   A WIND STAR

each division represents four days

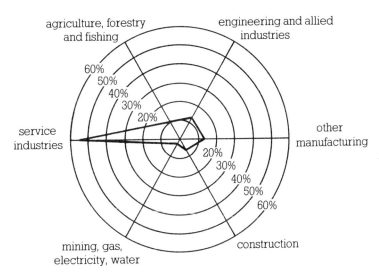

Fig 4.10   EMPLOYMENT IN LINCOLNSHIRE IN 1978 (FIGURES IN PERCENTAGES)

One aspect of weather studies is the direction of the wind (see page 32). Having recorded the wind direction over a period of time, it is necessary to process and display that information in some way. Fig 4.8 shows one way of doing this. Lines drawn to represent the points of the compass are divided into equal sections. These are used to draw a bar representing the number of days the wind has blown from that direction. From such a chart the most usual direction of the wind is easily noted.

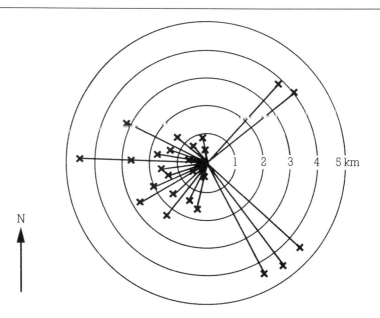

N

Fig 4.11   DIRECTION AND DISTANCE OF JOURNEYS TO A SPORTS CENTRE

If, instead of drawing bars, points are plotted on each of the direction lines and these are joined up, the diagram looks rather like a star (Fig 4.9).

Star diagrams like this can be used to display a variety of information. Fig 4.10 has a series of concentric circles drawn to make reading easier and it still has the radial lines, which now no longer represent direction. Such diagrams can have any number of radial lines equally spaced out.

A similar type of diagram may be used to show how far people travel to somewhere, whether it is a shopping centre, a workplace, a recreation area or some other place. The examples given in the diagrams are of a sports centre (Fig 4.11) and a shopping centre (Fig 4.12). In both cases the information came from a sample of people visiting the centre who answered questionnaires. The straight line distance and the direction of their homes from the centre was worked out from an Ordnance Survey map. Each plot represents one person, the concentric circles helping to place this accurately.

By studying the scale it can be seen that the people who visit the sports centre travel a much greater distance than those who come to the shopping centre. The shopping centre chart also shows one other piece of information – the method people use to travel to the centre.

It would be possible to plot this information on a map. However, the map may well obscure much of the information being plotted, and so a radial chart is more useful when analysing results. Map information can be transferred to a radial chart if required, as the diagram of open space in central Cambridge (Fig 4.13) shows.

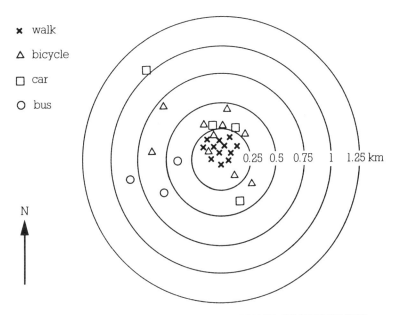

Fig 4.12   DIRECTION, DISTANCE AND METHOD OF TRAVEL FOR
JOURNEYS TO A SHOPPING CENTRE

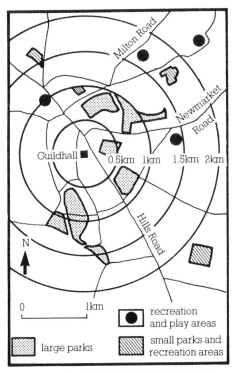

Fig 4.13   PUBLIC OPEN SPACE IN
CENTRAL CAMBRIDGE

1   Use the diagrams of wind
direction (Fig 4.8 and Fig 4.9) to
write down which is the main
wind direction in this area.
Which do you think is the most
useful of the two diagrams? Give
reasons for your answer.

2   (a) Make a list of the
differences between the
pattern of journeys people
make to the sports centre
(Fig 4.11) and to the shopping
centre (Fig 4.12).
(b) From the evidence in Fig
4.12, is there any pattern to
be seen? If so, how would you
investigate such a pattern in
more detail?

FINDING THE CONNECTION: 1
THE SCATTERGRAPH

Fieldwork is often undertaken in order to find a connection between two factors. For example, you may wish to find whether there is a connection between land use and altitude, or land use and slope, or land use and aspect, or soil, or geology. Having collected the data (see pages 87–8 for example), there is often so much in such a confused form that no connection can be seen.

One method of sorting out the information and finding whether there is a connection between the sets of data is to draw a graph. However, this graph cannot be a bar chart or histogram (see pages 109–10) because in this case there are two sets of information to compare.

The table in Fig 4.14 shows two sets of information, the amount of pastureland and the height at which it is found. This information was collected from a sample during a fieldwork investigation in Dyfed, Wales. The graph shows that the height of the land is plotted on the horizontal axis of the graph with the percentage of pastureland on the vertical axis. The height and amount of pastureland at each sample point is plotted with a cross on the graph.

When a line is drawn around the points which have been plotted, we can see from its shape whether there is a connection between, in this case, height and pastureland (see Fig 4.16).

This type of graph, known as a scattergraph, can be used to plot three factors. In the graph of travel to a shopping centre (Fig 4.15), the investigator was interested in finding a link between the distance travelled and the time taken. The idea was that people coming from a greater distance would not take a great deal longer because they would use a quicker form of transport. The graph shows that, instead of using a cross, the type of transport each person used is plotted on the graph and a key is provided.

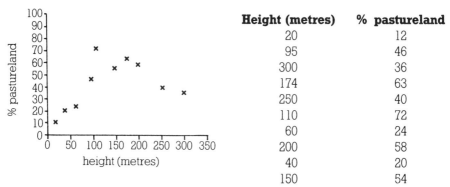

Height (metres)	% pastureland
20	12
95	46
300	36
174	63
250	40
110	72
60	24
200	58
40	20
150	54

Fig 4.14   TABLE AND SCATTERGRAPH OF THE HEIGHT AND % PASTURELAND IN PART OF DYFED

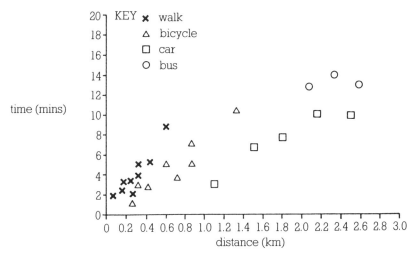

Fig 4.15 SCATTERGRAPH OF TRAVEL TO A SHOPPING CENTRE

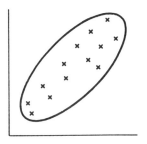

A high positive relationship

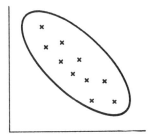

A high negative relationship

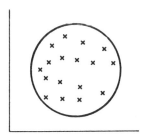

No relationship

Fig 4.16 DOES THE SCATTERGRAPH
SHOW A RELATIONSHIP?

1 Does the graph showing height and percentage of pastureland show that there is a connection?

2 Does the graph of travel to a shopping centre show:

(a) a connection between the length of time taken and the journey distance?

(b) any link between the journey distance and time and the type of transport used for the journey?

FINDING THE CONNECTION: 2
CORRELATION

It is possible to find whether there is a connection between two factors without drawing a graph. Imagine that the investigator has recorded the number of buses per day and the size of ten villages in north Cambridgeshire in order to test the idea that: larger villages have the best public bus services and that the service declines as village size decreases. This could provide data for part of a study of transport services in rural areas.

The data collected is displayed in a table (Fig 4.17), with one list giving size of village and the other giving number of buses. In order to discover whether there is a connection between village size and number of buses, each list should be placed in rank order. Rank order means that the list is put in order with the largest at the top and the smallest at the bottom (see Fig 4.18). When the two lists are placed side by side like this, lines are drawn connecting the same villages in each of the lists.

If the connection were perfect then none of the lines would cross because the two rank orders would be the same. By counting the number of times lines cross – it is a good idea to put a small coloured circle round each crossing – the investigator can find out how near to perfect the connection is. When the two orders are complete opposites there are 45 crossings if there are ten sets. If this is so, it shows that the idea is completely wrong and that bus services decline in number as villages get larger. A number of 5 to 10 crossings would show a connection, 35 to 40 would show an opposite connection.

To find the connection mathematically the two ranked lists may be used again. The formula is known as 'Spearman Rank Correlation' (the word 'correlation' really means connection) and is always given as:

$$r_s = 1 - \frac{6 \Sigma d^2}{N^3 - N}$$

r_s = Spearman Rank Correlation
Σ = the sum of
d = difference between the two ranks
N = number of ranks

Working this out for the data on population and buses, we first of all put each list in order as before. The difference between the two ranks (d) is then worked out, as in Fig 4.19, column 4. This is then squared in column 5 as the formula suggests. All these numbers are then added together (this is the meaning of Σ in the formula) and multiplied by 6. The top line of the formula has now been worked out and is 180.

For the bottom line of the formula, the number of ranks (N) is 10. So N^3 is 10^3 which is 1000, minus N which is $1000 - 10 = 990$. This gives the bottom line which is to be divided into 180. The answer, which is 0.18, is taken away from 1 to give the final answer, 0.82.

The nearer the answer is to 1, the better the connection between the two ranks.

Village	No. of buses per day	Population
Littleport	29	4810
Prickwillow	3	470
Stuntney	8	230
Barway	1	100
Wilburton	10	830
Haddenham	11	2050
Witcham	5	320
Mepal	7	540
Lt. Downham	6	1360
Aldreth	2	180

Fig 4.17   BUS FREQUENCY AND POPULATION OF TEN NORTH CAMBRIDGESHIRE VILLAGES

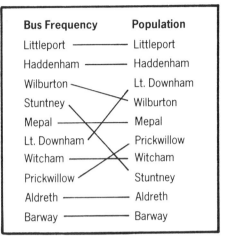

Fig 4.18   RANK ORDERS OF BUS FREQUENCY AND POPULATION

Village	Rank order of bus frequency	Rank order of population	Difference between rank orders (d)	Difference squared (d²)
Littleport	1	1	0	0
Prickwillow	8	6	2	4
Stuntney	4	8	4	16
Barway	10	10	0	0
Wilburton	3	4	1	1
Haddenham	2	2	0	0
Witcham	7	7	0	0
Mepal	5	5	0	0
Lt. Downham	6	3	3	9
Aldreth	9	9	0	0
			Total d^2 ($\Sigma\, d^2$)=30	

Fig 4.19   CORRELATION (SPEARMAN RANK CORRELATION COEFFICIENT) OF BUS FREQUENCY AND POPULATION

1   (a) Is there a connection between village size and the number of buses in north Cambridgeshire (i) shown in Fig 4.18? (ii) shown by the Spearman Rank Correlation? (b) How strong is this connection?

MAPPING

The question which geographers ask most is, 'Where?'. Many fieldwork investigations involve looking for patterns, for instance of housing types, building materials or function of buildings in a village, town or city, or of changing patterns of land use in a rural area. Although the main differences may be shown on a graph, the only way to give an overall impression of the pattern is to use a map.

Drawing maps is an extremely skilled technique and an investigator is unlikely to be able to draw a very accurate map without basing it on one already drawn. It may be possible to place data on a printed map. In such a case it is important to make sure that the data stands out clearly from the detail on the map. Data shown by colours on a black and white map could be successful.

However, often the published map which is being used contains so much printed information that it would obscure the information being put onto the map. In this case the investigator must draw a new base map. Tracing cabinets which are glass topped and have a light underneath make the job much easier. When tracing a base map it is only necessary to trace essential information.

	Small terraced pre World War 1 housing
	Larger terraced or semi-detached pre World War 1 housing
	Large pre World War 1 houses, set in their own grounds
	Modern council housing
	Modern privately owned housing of small or medium size
	Large modern detached or semi-detached houses
	Industry
	Shops
	Offices
P P P	Public buildings
	Recreational area
	Derelict/wasteland

Fig 4.20   KEY TO LAND USE MAP SHOWN OPPOSITE

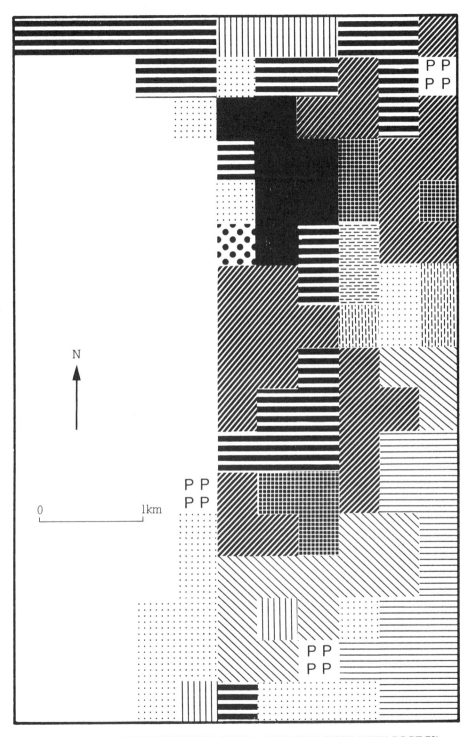

LAND USE OF PART OF WESTON-SUPER-MARE (COMPARE WITH PAGE 72)

PART 4: PROCESSING AND PRESENTING THE DATA

In map drawing it is important to make the map as clear and easy to read as possible. To help clarity, the map should not be so small that everything becomes jumbled up. Labelling should, as far as possible, be horizontal so that it can be read with the map the right way up. It is much better to print labels carefully on maps with a fine pen; this helps presentation and is easier to read. As few things as possible should be put in the key. On a map of land use, for example, it should not be necessary to put any other information in the key. It is also usual practice on a map to mark which is north and to give the scale of the map, so that the reader can quickly see the size of the area covered.

Colour shading on a map helps to make the information easier to read. If appropriate colours are chosen, this also makes reading easier. For some features there are colours which are commonly used: for instance, for land use the Land Utilization Survey colours could be used. But when deciding on a colour it is possible to choose colours which have some link with the data being presented.

Sometimes an investigator may wish to put two types of information on one map. For instance, it may be difficult to compare geology or soils on one map with land use on another map. In this case the information on geology or soil could be marked on the base map. The land use could then be marked on tracing paper placed over the base map. When finished the 'tracing overlay' could be placed carefully over the base map and stuck down along one edge. The two sets of information can then be compared through the tracing (see Fig 4.21).

1 Which colours would you use to show function of buildings on the map of Weston-Super-Mare on page 120?
2 How would you map building materials from the evidence collected in the village of Reach (page 65)? You will first need to decide on the combinations of walls and roof, e.g. brick and tile, brick and slate, etc. and then on appropriate colours.

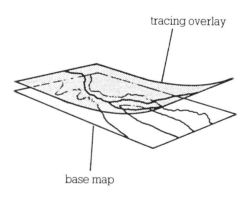

tracing overlay

base map

Fig 4.21   USING A TRACING OVERLAY

HOW MANY ARE THERE?
DOT AND DENSITY MAPS

~ Parish boundary

• Each dot represents
   one pupil

N

0   2km

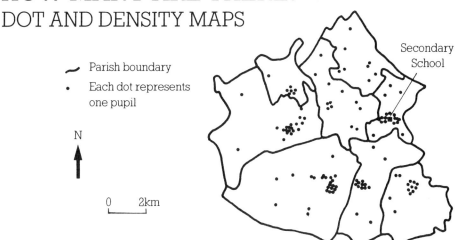

Secondary
School

Fig 4.22   LOCATION OF HOMES OF PUPILS MOVING FROM THEIR
FIRST SCHOOL TO A SECONDARY SCHOOL

~ Parish boundary

• One dot represents
   100 people

N

0   2km

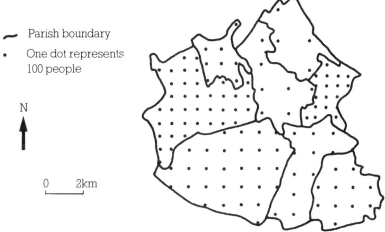

Fig 4.23   POPULATION OF SELECTED PARISHES

Have you ever noticed how crowded some parts of a town are
compared with others? A look at a map will show how some rural
areas have more houses than others. Geographers are interested in
why there are more people or houses, or more of one crop than
another, or more sheep or cattle in one area than another, and in how
they are distributed or positioned in an area.

Fig 4.22 shows where the pupils moving to a secondary school from
their first school will come from. There is one dot for each pupil and
this is positioned where the pupil lives. The map shows how the
pupils' homes are spread around the school.

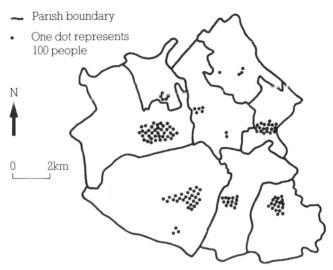

Parish boundary

One dot represents
100 people

N

0   2km

Fig 4.24   POPULATION OF SELECTED PARISHES
(COMPARE WITH Fig 4.23)

These pupils come from a rural area and the total number of people living in each parish is shown in Fig 4.23. This map would be much too crowded if each person were represented by one dot, so each dot represents 100 persons. It would be very difficult to position the dots in the centre of where each group of 100 people lives, so they are positioned evenly throughout the parish. However, it may be better to place them where settlements appear on a map, as shown in Fig 4.24.

Some parishes are more crowded than others. Geographers need to know how crowded an area is: they call this the 'density' of population and it is usually given as density per square kilometre, although the unit of area may vary. Page 58 gave details of the number of people living in wards within the city of Cambridge. These details could be shown by using dots. The wards which are most crowded would have more dots and would look darker on the map. This idea of showing more crowded areas with darker shading is used when drawing a 'density shading map' (see Fig 4.25).

To construct this map the density of population for each area (in this case wards) was worked out by dividing the number of people by the area of the ward in hectares or square kilometres. This gave figures ranging from 11.1 to 74.01 persons per hectare. Four equal divisions were chosen (there could be more or less) and each was given a type of shading in the key. Notice how the shading for the highest density is the darkest, and how the shadings look lighter as the density is less. It is usual to use black or another single colour for this. Trying to use different colours is very difficult and usually fails to give a good impression.

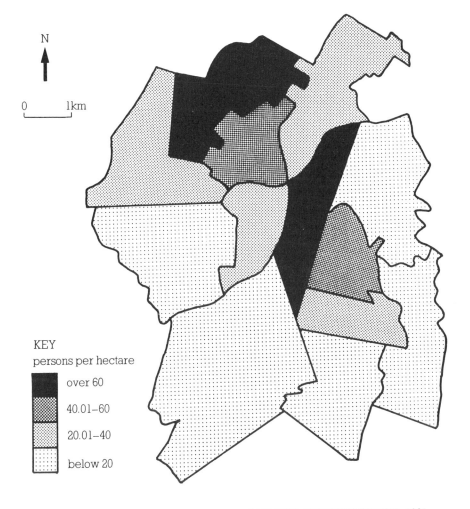

KEY
persons per hectare

■	over 60
▦	40.01–60
░	20.01–40
·	below 20

Fig 4.25   CAMBRIDGE: DENSITY OF POPULATION BY WARDS, 1981

1   Choose which of Fig 4.23 and Fig 4.24 you think best illustrates:
(a) the number of people living in each parish,
(b) which parish has the highest density of population.
2   Using the information for either 1961 or 1971 from page 58, trace an outline map of wards and show by density shading the density of population for the chosen year. Remember to work out the density of population first and then, for this exercise, choose five divisions and shadings for the key.

LINE MAPS
ISOLINE MAPS

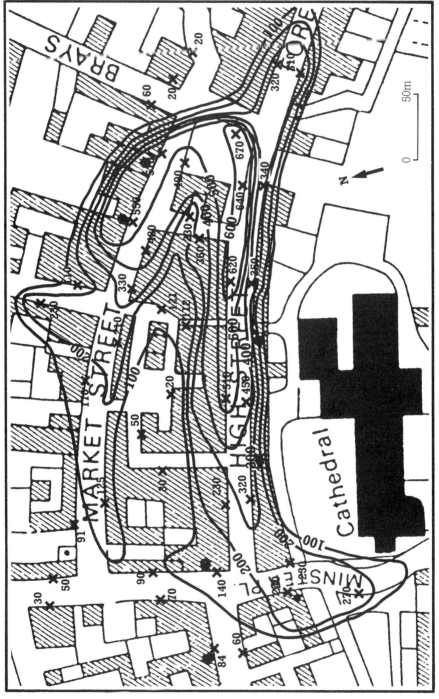

Fig 4.26   ISOLINE MAP OF RESULTS FROM A STATIC PEDESTRIAN COUNT CARRIED OUT IN ELY TOWN CENTRE (2.30 p.m. – 3.00 p.m. SATURDAY AUGUST 27, 1983)

Geographers often ask questions like these:
'is there a change of temperature as the distance from a school increases? (see page 31);
'is there a change in the number of pedestrians as the distance from the peak land value intersection increases?' (see pages 79–80);
'is there a change in the number of buses as the distance from the city centre increases?' (see pages 97–8).

The information required to answer such questions can be collected for a series of points around the school or centre. This information can then be recorded on a map as numbers at these points. However, these numbers do not make a pattern. A pattern can be produced by drawing lines joining points with the same value. However, a quick look at the figures collected during any one of the above investigations will show that only a small number of points have the same value.

The first thing to do to tackle this problem and draw a line (or isoline) map is to decide which number interval to choose. For example, in the case of the investigation into temperature, the figures range from 12.6 to 15.4°C. As the lines which are to be drawn should be at equal intervals, six lines could be drawn, ranging from 12.5 to 15.0°C. In the case of the investigation into numbers of pedestrians, the figures range from 20 to 670, and an interval of 100 would give six lines ranging from 100 to 600.

Having decided on the interval, the lines can then be drawn. It can be seen from the maps that only a few of the points have the same value as the lines. If a line is started at a figure with the same value as the line then it is a matter of judgement how near to go to a lower or higher number. The completed map, however, will help to answer the questions that were asked.

---

1 Choose a line on the map opposite and follow it round the centre – notice how it goes between numbers which are higher or lower than the value of the line.
2 From the information shown on the map, how would you answer the second question at the top of this page?
3 Use a piece of tracing paper to trace from the map on page 98 the position of Ely and the values for the number of buses. Then:
    (a) choose the value at which lines (isolines) could be drawn – remember to choose equal intervals.
    (b) draw in the isolines on the traced map at the intervals you have chosen.
    (c) use this evidence to discuss whether there is a change in the number of buses as the distance from the city increases. What change do you notice?

PART 4: PROCESSING AND PRESENTING THE DATA

MAPPING FLOWS

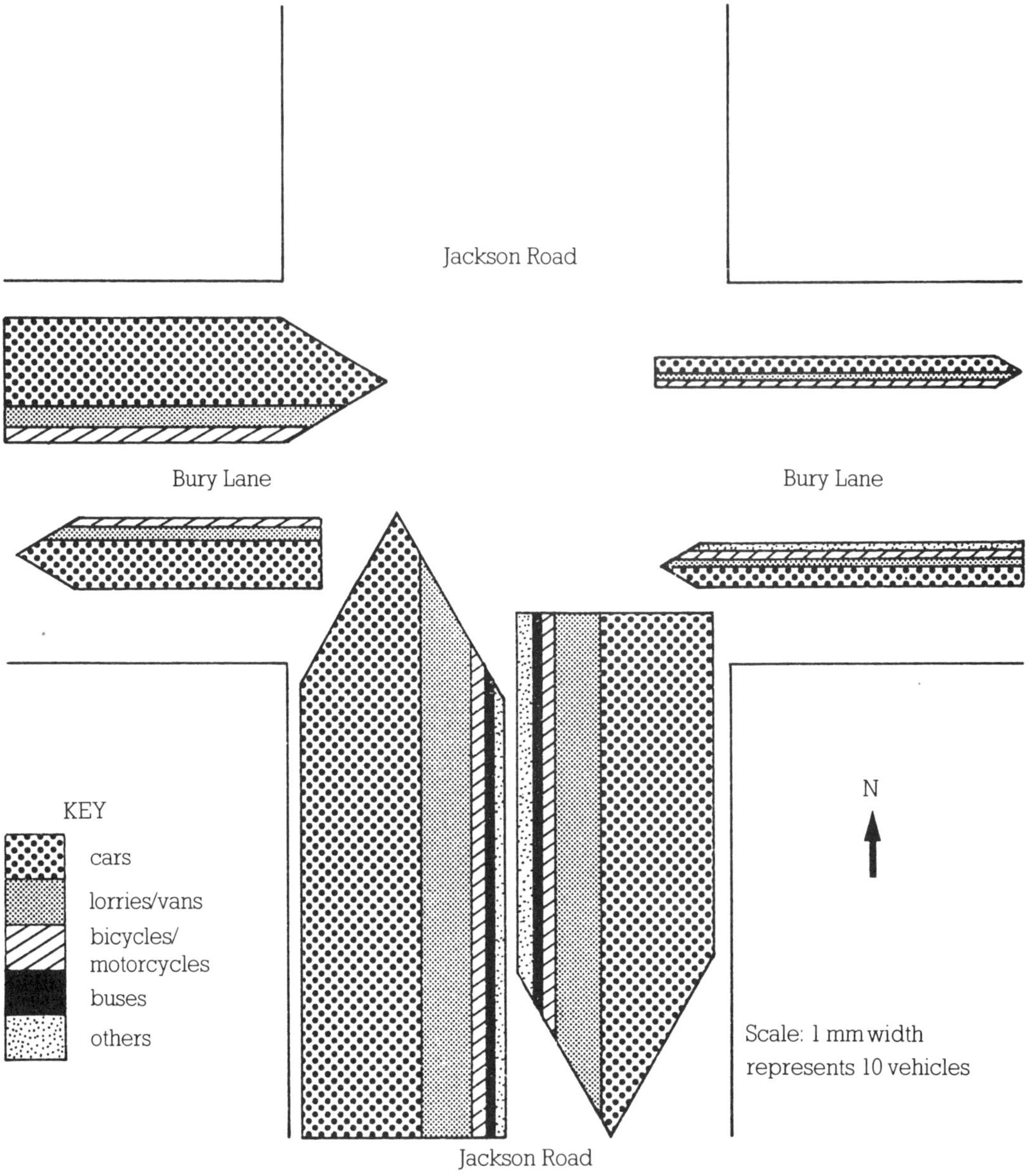

Jackson Road

Bury Lane

Bury Lane

KEY

- cars
- lorries/vans
- bicycles/ motorcycles
- buses
- others

N

Scale: 1 mm width represents 10 vehicles

Jackson Road

	Cars	Lorries/vans	Bicycles/ motorcycles	Buses	Others
Jackson Road (travelling N)	105	77	22	10	10
Jackson Road (travelling S)	125	54	25	10	15

Fig 4.27   TYPES OF VEHICLE AT INTERSECTION OF JACKSON ROAD AND BURY LANE

Many investigations which geographers undertake involve movement. Pedestrians moving along a pavement and traffic or buses travelling along a road are two examples. This movement can be mapped.

The method of mapping involves drawing an arrow which points in the direction of movement of the flow. This may be a straight arrow or it could be bent along the route being followed. However, in the latter case this can often lead to very complicated drawing.

The width or thickness of the arrow is used to show the amount of the traffic flow; this can be seen in the map of pedestrian flows shown in Fig 4.28. It is very important that the scale is chosen with care. The final arrows should not be so thick that they obscure the map, nor so thin that differences cannot be seen. It is a good idea to draw the arrow with the highest number and the one with the lowest number on scraps of paper first to see how the final arrows will look.

In some cases, such as that of traffic flow at an intersection, the arrows can be divided up to show the different types of vehicle travelling along a road. In Fig 4.27 the fieldworker was investigating whether certain roads carried particular types of traffic. As part of the investigation, this traffic flow map at one important intersection was drawn.

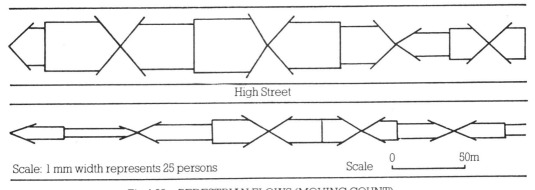

High Street

Scale: 1 mm width represents 25 persons

Scale 0 ⌞_____⌟ 50m

Fig 4.28   PEDESTRIAN FLOWS (MOVING COUNT)

1   You will notice that one arrow at the intersection in Fig 4.27 has not been drawn. The figures for it are shown in the table beneath the diagram.

(a) Take a piece of tracing paper and on it draw the edges of the roads at the intersection.

(b) On your tracing paper draw the traffic flow arrows for Jackson Road, using the figures given here.

(c) Discuss with your friend how far these results show that certain roads carry particular types of traffic, and how the recorder should continue the investigation.

2   Look at Fig 4. 28 which shows the results of a moving pedestrian count taken in a town centre. What does this diagram show about the numbers of pedestrians moving on each side of the street? Attempt to explain the things you notice.

THE FINAL ACT

Writing up the fieldwork is an important part of the whole project. The first section should be concerned with the background information which helped to provide the setting for the work. Material collected in the early stages of investigation can be used here. This should lead to a statement of the ideas to test (hypotheses) or the questions being asked. These should be written out clearly and broken down into testable sections.

The second section should contain a description of how the investigation was carried out. This will include information about how each idea was tested and the equipment which was used. At this point the reasons should be given for the decisions made about the methods: for example, why particular positions were chosen when a pedestrian count was undertaken, or the time of day chosen for a traffic count. If a sampling technique was used, then the reasons for using it should be outlined in this section.

A third section should contain the graphs, maps, diagrams and sketches which show the results of each of the surveys which were undertaken. As each is drawn, a description of the main points which it shows should be given. This represents the evidence which has been collected to test the hypothesis and should be as accurate as possible.

Finally, the conclusion should weigh up all the evidence which has been collected to test each smaller idea. At this point it is important to be honest – if the evidence does not show what was expected, then it is of little value trying to say that it does. Perhaps the evidence shows the opposite of what was expected. This is still very useful and interesting. All the investigator can do at this stage is to say what was found as a result of the work. Having tested each smaller idea, the evidence can be used to test the main hypothesis.

After all the work, it may well be that the results are inconclusive and a clear cut decision about whether the hypothesis has been proved or not cannot be made. In such a case, it may be worthwhile to give some reasons why this may be so, and to suggest some further investigations which could be undertaken to give a more conclusive outcome.

THE PROJECT OUTLINE

SECTION 1   The Hypotheses
- background information
- the reasons for the investigation
- the ideas to test (hypotheses)

SECTION 2   The Method
- the method used to investigate each hypothesis
- the equipment used
- the decisions about where, how and why particular methods were used, e.g. sampling technique

SECTION 3   The Results
- the maps, diagrams, graphs or sketches showing the results of each investigation
  a description of what each shows

SECTION 4   The Conclusion
- testing each hypothesis in turn using the evidence collected
- how far the main hypothesis is shown to be proved
- ideas for further investigation

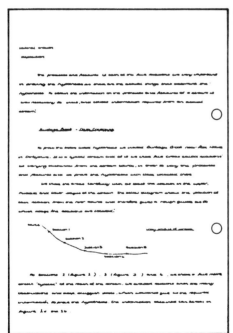
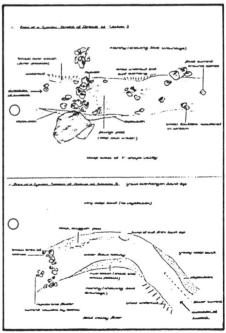

PAGES FROM A STUDY OF A STREAM. BY LESLEY BURGESS, CITY SCHOOL, SHEFFIELD

COMPLETION AND GENERAL PRESENTATION

After all the hard work that has gone into a piece of fieldwork, it is worthwhile taking a little time to present the results properly.

At the beginning there should be a title page. This should contain the title of the work: in most cases the main idea or hypothesis being tested will act as the title. Of course, the author's name should appear there also, as should the date when the work was completed. If the work is to be presented for examination you should ask the teacher whether any other information should be included.

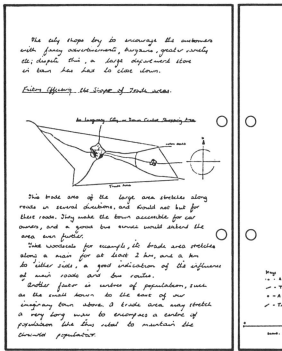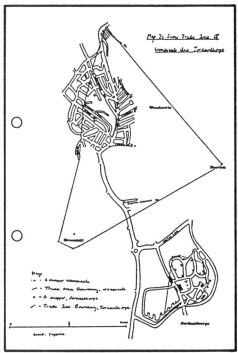

PAGES FROM A STUDY CONCERNING SHOPPING CENTRES IN SHEFFIELD.
BY ALISTAIR SMITH, GLEADLESS VALLEY SCHOOL, SHEFFIELD

Following the title page should come the contents page. This should include the main sections of the work. It is difficult to lay down hard and fast rules, but this page should give a good indication of what the work contains. It should not contain details of every page. The contents could be divided into sections such as 'background', 'the hypothesis', 'method', 'results', 'conclusion'. Page numbers should be included. This will involve numbering all the pages of the work, including those which contain diagrams, sketches or maps. If, however, a large map or model is included, then this could be presented separately. An optional extra would be to list the diagrams, sketches, maps, etc. as figures, giving each a figure number which could be referred to in the writing, along with the page number.

It is not necessary to have a piece of work typed, so long as the writing is clear. Always try to be as precise as possible and avoid long sentences. It is important to write clearly, but the real purpose of the study is not an essay but a geography fieldwork investigation. When referring to maps or diagrams, graphs or sketches, it gets rather tedious to keep referring to them by their full title. It is often better, having given the title once, to give the figure number, numbering from first to last.

Well presented maps and diagrams can really add to the value of a piece of work. Colour should be used wherever necessary; each diagram should have a title and should be carefully and accurately drawn. Often, however, it is the labelling which spoils an otherwise good piece of work; printed labelling is preferable to writing. The labelling should be kept horizontal wherever possible, to avoid the reader having to twist the page in order to read it.

At the end of the work there should be a bibliography. This is a list of all the books, pamphlets, and other printed materials that have been used. This should be laid out with the name of the author of each work first, followed by the date the work was published, the title and the publisher. Anyone else reading the work and wanting to find the publication can then trace it easily. The authors' names should be in alphabetical order.

The completed work can be presented in a folder; a card folder with a treasury tag to hold the papers would be suitable. With the title and author on the front, this will be an ideal way to present what is a piece of original research.

1 Write out an imaginary title page and contents list for a piece of research you would like to undertake.

2 Choose any three books from the classroom or library shelves and list them as you would for a bibliography.

SOURCES OF INFORMATION

PART OF THE CAMBRIDGESHIRE LOCAL COLLECTION

The majority of fieldwork studies are concerned with relatively small areas. Consequently many of the most useful sources of information are those produced locally. These will probably be found either in the Local Collection, which is usually housed in the local library (see pages 27–8), or in the Local Records Office. In both cases specific information should be asked for, rather than a general request for all you have about . . .'. These collections usually hold large amounts of material and it is almost impossible for the librarian or curator to find useful material from such a general request.

Much of the material held at a local library collection will be historical: old photographs, newspapers, posters, papers and books. There may be histories written by local people. Such material may be useful for studies which are looking at the way in which an area has changed. Kelly's Directory is one historical source which may prove useful; it contains a wealth of detail, particularly that related to occupations and businesses in a town or village. In addition, there could well be local planning studies, looking at leisure, housing or transport, which could be used for background material.

One major source, particularly for the geographer, is maps (see page 25). As well as the standard maps of an area, there are other specialist maps for certain areas. The Ordnance Survey publishes geological maps on behalf of the Institute of Geological Sciences and the Soil Survey of England and Wales. These are available for almost the whole of Britain. Soil maps on the other hand are only available for certain areas, as are the Land Utilization Survey maps which show land use. By law the local planning authority is required to produce maps showing proposed developments in its area. These maps show functions such as retailing, industry, residential areas, open space and a variety of other features. They are revised regularly and are open for inspection at the local planning offices.

A wealth of statistical information exists, but much of it is for large areas of the country and can only provide background material. The census contains information for a range of different sized areas. For local studies, information for individual wards and parishes may be useful. The smallest area for which details are available is the enumeration district, which is usually only a few streets. This material contains statistics on the housing types and quality of the housing, as well as population figures, the age-sex structure, birthplaces and occupations. The information available at each census may change slightly, as may the boundary of the survey area. Obviously, when the ward or district boundary changes for census purposes, the areas are different and cannot be compared. However, it may well be worth discussing the problem with someone who may be able to suggest a solution.

Probably the greatest sources of information are the people with specialist knowledge: the geography teachers, the librarians, and others such as planners, who may help. Serious requests for information and assistance are never turned down – it is well worth asking. The other source is, of course, the area where the study is to take place; it is the fieldworker who will be the most valuable source of all.

Fig 4.29   DISCUSSION WITH A TEACHER
            OFTEN HELPS . . . .

INDEX

acidity (soil) 43–4
aspect 16,39,62

bar chart 108,109–10
beach 53–6
  profile 55
Beaufort Scale 30
bedload 52
bibliography 132
book (outline) 4
buildings
  age 66,69–71
  function 66,76–8
  height 79
  material 66
  style 66,69–71
  survey 26,65
bus
  frequency 85–6,98,109–10, 118
  timetable 97–8

census 27,57,59–61,134
  small area statistics 59
Central Business District 76–82
  building height 76
  functions 76–8
  Peak Land Value Intersection 79
choice 7–8
cities 74–84
  Central Business District 76
  transect 74–5
cliffs 53
climate 32–3
clinometer 40,45,53
clipboard 13
clothing 2
coasts 53–6
  beach profile 55
  cliffs 53
  longshore drift 55
  waves 53–4
colour (soil) 43
colour (use of) 121,132
Common Seablite 56
conclusion 129
connection (finding a) 115–18

contents page 131–2
correlation 117–18
Country Code 14
countryside 105–6
  pressures 105–6
crop survey 26
current meter 48

density
  maps 122–4
  pedestrian 79–80,82
  population 57
directories 91
discharge (river) 48–50
distribution 57
dot maps 122–4

enumeration district 134
environmental quality 101–2
  rural 101–2
  urban 101–4
equipment 2–3
evaporation 35
evaporation pan 35–6

factory 93–4
farm 89–90
  input/output 89
  checklist 90
fieldwork 1
  reasons for 5
  steps to take 5–6
floats 49
flow diagram 86,94,127–8
flow lines 86,97
frontage (shop) 82
function 64–6, 74–8

geology 62,87
gradient 41

height (slope) 39
histogram 109–10
horizon (soil) 42
humus 42
hypothesis 129–32
hypsometer 45–6

ideas 4,7–10
industry 91–4
  checklist 93
  classification 91
  flow diagram 94
  input/output 94
  survey 91–2
infiltration 36–8
  rate 17,36
interception 34–5
interview 15,19,21,90,93
isolines 31,79,97,125–6

Kelly's Directory 60,92,133

labelling 121,132
land use (rural) 87–8,89–90
  categories 88
  recording 87
land use (urban) 71–3,120
library 27–8,133–4
line maps 125–6
load (river) 50–2
  bedload 52
  solution load 51
  suspended sediment 51
Local Collection 28,57,133–4
Local Records Office 133
Local Studies 27
longshore drift 55

mapping 119–28
  density maps 122–4
  dot maps 122–4
  drawing 119–21
  flows 127–8
  overlay 121
  shading 199–20
  tracing 119
maps 25–6,27,134
mean 107–8
median 107–8
mode 107–8

neighbourhood 99–100
  mapping 100
newspapers 85,133

outline (of project) 130

pantometer 41
parish registers 57
parking (cars) 106
passenger car unit 95–6
Peak Land Value Intersection 79
pebbleometer 51–2
pedestrian count 79–80
  flow 128
  moving count 80
  static count 79,125
photocopy 27
photographs 23–4
pie chart 111
population 57–61
  change 59–61
  mapping 122–4
  pyramids 61
position 63
precipitation 34,36
presentation 131–2
primary sources 15

quadrat 47,56
questionnaire 19–22,67–8,85,90

radial chart 112–14
railways 97
rainfall 34–7
  intensity 35
rain gauge 34,36
ranging rod 55
rating curve 49
registration numbers (cars) 97
relief 62
retailing 83–4
rivers 48–52
  cross sectional area 49
  discharge 48–9
  load 50–2
  velocity 48–9
roundness index 56
rural area 25,87–8

sampling   17–18,74,87–8
  line   17–18
  random   17–18
  systematic   17–18
scattergraph   115–16
Sea Beet   55
Sea Purslane   56
secondary sources   15
sediment sampler   50
services   64
shopping centres   18,83–4
  hierarchy   83
  quality   104
shops   76–84
  customer count   82
  frontage   82
  grouping   82
  hypermarket   83
site   62–3
sketch   23,63
sketch map   62
slopes   39–41
  angle of steepness   40
  aspect   16,39,62
  height   39
soil   42–4,63
  acidity   43–4
  auger   42
  colour   43
  horizon   42
  moisture content   38
  profile   42
  texture   43
Spearman Rank Correlation   117–18
star diagram   112–14
statement   9–10
stemflow   35–6
streetscape   103–4
survey
  building   26,65
  crops   26
  land use   71–3,87–8
suspended sediment   51

telephone directory   85,91
temperature   29–31
texture (soil)   43
thermometer   29
tourists   5,105–6
towns   69–73
  building style   69–70
  growth   69
  land use   71–3
traffic   95–8
  census   95,106
  flow   97–8, 127–8
  passenger car unit   95–6
  recording   96
transect   74,87
transpiration   34
transport   95–8

urban field   85

vegetation   45–7
  frequency   46–7
  spread   46
  stratification   45
velocity (river)   48–9
village   62–8
  buildings   65–8
  change   64–8
  function   64
  growth   64–8
  position   63
  site   62–3

wards   57–8, 134
water supply   62
waves   53–4
weather   29–34
weather vane   30
whirling psychrometer   30–1
wind   30,32
  measurement   30,32
  rose   112
  star   112
writing up   129–32
work   91–4